Key Stage 2

Second Resource Book

(relating to National Curriculum Levels 3 and 4)

Alan Brighouse / David Godber / Peter Patilla

Nelson

Thomas Nelson and Sons Ltd
Nelson House   Mayfield Road
Walton-on-Thames   Surrey
KT12 5PL   UK

51 York Place
Edinburgh EH1 3JD   UK

Thomas Nelson (Hong Kong) Ltd
Toppan Building 10/F
22A Westlands Road
Quarry Bay   Hong Kong

Distributed in Australia by

Thomas Nelson Australia
102 Dodds Street
South Melbourne   Victoria 3205

Nelson Canada
1120 Birchmount Road   Scarborough
Ontario M1K 5G4   Canada

© **A. Brighouse, D. Godber, P. Patilla 1989**

First published by Thomas Nelson and Sons Ltd 1989

ISBN 0-17-421548-7

NPN 9 8 7 6 5

Filmset in the Nelson Teaching Alphabet
by Mould Type Foundry Ltd
Dunkirk Lane   Leyland   England

Printed in Hong Kong

Design   Sharon Platt, Colin Reed, Linda Reed
Photography   Chris Ridgers
Illustration   Colin Reed

Photographic props by courtesy of E J Arnold Ltd, Hestair Hope Ltd, and ESA Ltd
The classroom scenes were photographed in Kingston Road Middle School, Staines and St. Anne's Primary School, Basingstoke and the publishers would like to thank the teachers and pupils for their co-operation.

Contents

Introduction
Peak mathematics: the materials (relating to National Curriculum Levels 3 to 6)

Peak mathematics provides structure and continuity of mathematics from Level 1 to Level 6 of the National curriculum.

The part of the scheme covering National Curriculum Levels 3 to 6 is organised as five Resource Books for teachers, supported by a variety of pupil materials. This book covers material for children at Levels 3 and 4. The range of materials for Levels 3 to 6 is shown in the following table. The Level numbers in heavy type show the main focus of the listed materials.

Level	Pupil materials	Teacher materials
2 **3** 4	Peak Zero Peak One part 1 Peak One part 2 Number Skills One Peak Plus 1 Peak Explorer One part 1 Peak Explorer One part 2 Calculator Book	First Resource Book Peak Plus Teacher's Book 1 First Junior Progress Record Junior Assessment Zero Junior Assessment One part 1 Junior Assessment One part 2
3 4	Peak Two part 1 Peak Two part 2 Number Skills Two Peak Plus 2 Peak Explorer Two part 1 Peak Explorer Two part 2	Second Resource Book Peak Plus Teacher's Book 2 Second Junior Progress Record Junior Assessment Two part 1 Junior Assessment Two part 2
4 5	Peak Three parts 1 and 2 Number Skills Three Peak Plus 3 Peak Explorer Three	Third Resource Book Peak Plus Teacher's Book 3 Third Junior Progress Record Junior Assessment Three parts 1 and 2
4 5	Peak Four parts 1 and 2 Number Skills Four Peak Plus 4 Peak Explorer Four	Fourth Resource Book Peak Plus Teacher's Book 4 Fourth Progress Record Junior Assessment Four parts 1 and 2
4 **5** 6	Peak Extra	Extra Resource Book Extra Progress Record Assessment Extra parts 1 and 2
3–6	Peak Posters	Peak Posters Teacher's Notes

By the age of seven, some children will have progressed to the above materials, whereas others may require earlier Peak materials relating to Level 1 and Level 2 of the National Curriculum. This overlap is inevitable and where Infant and Junior schools are separate, it should be borne in mind when implementing the scheme.

Ideas for use alongside the activities in the Pupils' Books are detailed in each Resource Book.

Pupils' Books

The first pupil book in this part of the scheme is *Peak Zero*, which deals principally with the concept of place value. *Peak One* is split into two books (part 1 and part 2) and *Peak Two* is similarly split as we feel it is preferable for the younger children to break the year's work into two shorter books. Apart from the extra flexibility this allows in classroom organisation, the children will not be overwhelmed by the amount of work to be faced at each stage. *Peak Three* and *Peak Four* are each single books, sub-divided into two parts. *Peak Extra* is available to extend children who reach the end of *Peak Four*.

Number Skills books

These books provide an opportunity to apply acquired Number and Algebra skills in a range of different mathematical situations in order to consolidate and further develop a facility with Number and Algebra. The numbering of these books indicates the Pupils' Books to which they relate. However, they are not intended to be worked through systematically but rather to be used selectively as the need arises.

Peak Explorers

These workbooks consolidate a wide range of mathematical skills. They can be used alongside other **peak mathematics** pupils' materials of a similar level.

Peak Plus books

This series of books, numbered to relate to the other pupils' materials, allows the children to develop the techniques and strategies needed to solve puzzles, carry out investigations and play mathematical games. The activities in *Peak Plus* are predominantly those where the answer is of less importance than the method of working. The real purpose is to give the children confidence to think for themselves. The *Peak Plus* books extend work of a similar nature found in the main Pupils' Books, and focus on Attainment Targets 1 and 9. They allow ample opportunity for children to become involved in open-ended tasks and extended pieces of work across a range of topics.

Posters

These large posters have similar aims to the *Peak Plus* series. They are suitable for display, especially in 'investigation corners' in a school.

Progress Records

These are provided so that the teacher can summarise and monitor each child's progress. They are ideal for passing on to another teacher as the child completes a stage of Primary work. They can also be passed on to another school to give background information on the child's progress in mathematics.

Assessments

These are included in each of the Pupils' Books and are also available in the form of a tear-off pad. They can be used to check whether a child is ready to proceed to the next part of the scheme. The assessments may show areas where a child needs further help before he or she proceeds to new work. (For further comments on testing see pages 12 and 98 in this Resource Book.)

Curriculum areas covered in Peak materials (relating to National Curriculum Levels 3 to 6)

Number and Algebra

From work in Level 1 and in the Peak scheme, the child should have acquired the language and symbolism associated with Number. He or she should also have developed a sound understanding of numbers up to 20 and of all types of number bonds. Also, number line work and associated activities should have led to a knowledge of numbers up to 100.

In this part of the scheme, i.e. relating to National Curriculum Levels 3 to 6, the main emphasis initially is on place value work, which is introduced by use of structured apparatus before the child proceeds to formal Number operations. Activities involving other multibase structured apparatus besides denary have not been formally included in the scheme for teaching place value, although it is recognised that they can be beneficial. However, notes on the use of multibase materials for this purpose can be found in the *First Resource Book*. The suggested activities should be done prior to *Peak Zero*, which contains activities relating to place value and an understanding of the denary system. Once place value has been established, the formal operations are introduced in a carefully graded way. Each new step of the different processes is supported by practical experience and should be thoroughly understood before it is applied.

In each formal operation, there are three general steps to be considered:

1 understanding the operation
2 acquiring the skill
3 applying the skill to problem solving, open-ended tasks and puzzles.

The scheme provides a thorough grounding in the first step before requiring the child to tackle steps 2 and 3.

Work on Money runs alongside that on Number and Algebra and similar care has been taken to ensure that the children acquire an understanding of the monetary system. By the end of *Peak Two*, the children should be able to understand and apply the formal operations in Number and Money and the later books are increasingly concerned with their application to problems of all types, often involving the use of a calculator.

Fraction work is developed from the early activities of a practical nature which illustrate the equivalences involved. Decimal work is similarly introduced. The availability of the calculator in this work allows the use of an investigational approach in some of the decimal activities.

The *Number Skills* books allow the children to practise, consolidate and apply skills in Number and Algebra. Each book contains a variety of computational exercises, problems and puzzles.

In much of the Number work included in the scheme, the children are encouraged to decide whether the computation involved should be done:

1 mentally
2 by using a calculator
3 by a written approach
4 by any combination of the three methods above.

Measures   Earlier experience in Measures in **peak mathematics** involved the children in conservation activities from which precise language and the eventual need of units of measurement were derived. At such an early age, the standard units of measurement are unsuitable and it was necessary to involve the children in activities which afforded measuring experience but which used a range of personal and arbitrary units (for example, spans, cupfuls, ribbons) which are more suitable. This work should have extended the children's use of the language of measurement and offered experience in the following:

1 estimation – an indication that the value of the units being used is appreciated
2 choice of arbitrary units – an indication that the children can choose sensible units for different tasks
3 approximation – an indication that the level of precision required for a particular task is appreciated.

The children are now ready for experience with standard units. Such experience should be of a practical nature initially (*Peak One*). The aims outlined during the work with arbitrary units should still be borne in mind during the early work with standard units.

As the children acquire the relevant measurement skills, the opportunity will arise to use them for solving problems. Some of these will be of a practical nature, perhaps concerned with things the children find about them in their everyday lives.

Time   By now the children should be familiar with the general vocabulary of time (days of the week, months, the calendar, etc.) and the major intervals of time (for example, o'clock, $\frac{1}{4}$ past, $\frac{1}{2}$ past, $\frac{1}{4}$ to). In the scheme, the children will gain experience in five aspects of time:

1 the concepts of time (timing devices, timing of events and activities)
2 functional time (informal time language such as bedtime, tomorrow, early)
3 calendars and special days (festivals, seasons, months)
4 telling the time (oral aspect)
5 reading and recording time (24 hour clock, timetables).

Shape and space   Through earlier experience the children should have met a range of shapes, both natural and geometric and explored their texture and the patterns they make. The work now progresses to further exploration of all types of shapes in a practical way, some of the work lending itself to an investigative approach.

The children will be involved in:

1 sorting and classifying 2D and 3D shapes using a variety of criteria and apparatus
2 constructing 2D and 3D shapes
3 tessellation activities using a variety of media
4 a consideration of symmetry
5 investigating patterns and properties of shapes
6 specifying locations by use of co-ordinates
7 exploring angles.

Handling data The idea of representing information pictorially should be familiar to the children as a result of previous experience of collecting and processing a variety of data. This experience is now further developed by the introduction of other methods of handling data often involving the use of scale.

Content within the books

The scheme is designed to allow maximum flexibility of use within the classroom and to permit each child, or group of children, to proceed at an appropriate pace without interfering with the progress of others. A broad outline of the planning within the books is shown below.

Peak Zero This book deals mainly with place value, leading to the formal operation of addition of Number. It initially demands of the children a sound understanding of number bond work up to 20 and proceeds to develop an appreciation of place value through the use of structured apparatus.

As an understanding of the denary system and the equivalences involved develops, the formal operation of addition is introduced to ensure that the children can apply the principles of place value. Other formal Number operations are introduced in later books.

Assessment pages are included at the end of the book to show whether the teaching points have been understood.

Peak One In *Peak One* and *Peak Two* the contents of the book are divided into small modules
Peak Two of work each relating to one of the four major areas of mathematics, namely Number and Algebra, Measures, Shape and space and Handling data. The modules of work within a book may be done in any order; each is independent and will not involve concepts developed elsewhere in the same book. However, each concept developed will be exploited fully in the following book. Hence the need to complete one book before proceeding to the next one. We hope that this flexibility will allow teachers greater freedom when organising mathematics lessons and that it will be easier to group and regroup children, if desired.

The work within each module is progressive, and it is essential that a child works through it sequentially. This is equally true of work relating to the operations of Number, where the examples are carefully graded in order of difficulty and are based on the levels of skill that have been acquired at each stage.

Peak Three In *Peak Three*, *Peak Four* and *Peak Extra* the work on each main area of
Peak Four mathematics is spread through the book and is often of a more general nature.
Peak Extra

In all Pupils' Books, the apparatus required for each activity is shown at the top of the page. This apparatus should be assembled beforehand so it is readily available for the children. An apparatus list showing the total requirements for *Peak Two* is given on page 99.

At the end of each Pupils' Book is a glossary of new terms which can be used as a valuable point of reference.

The care with which the scheme has been written ensures a sound mathematical development for the children working through it. To a large extent this relieves the teacher of the problem of planning such a course and providing all the ideas required. However, the scheme depends upon the teacher being actively involved at all stages: with the implementation of the scheme; in good organisation and planning; in effective marking; in assessment and consequent discussion with each child or group of children. The scheme also allows teachers to supplement the material by developing the activities suggested in this book and by incorporating environmental mathematics, where appropriate. Indeed, the scheme in no way precludes teachers from adding their own material as they see fit.

Suggestions for further activities suitable for use alongside the Pupils' Books are detailed in each relevant Resource Book.

Content Matrix: Peak Zero to Peak Extra
(relating to National Curriculum Levels 3 to 6)

		Peak Zero	Peak One part 1	Peak One part 2
NUMBER AND ALGEBRA	Notation	Equivalence of tens and units. Abacus work	Value of digits in numbers. Abacus work	Reading of intermediate points on various scales. Digit values
	Addition	Addition of tens and units	Addition of hundreds, tens and units	Addition of hundreds, tens and units. Using, applying and consolidating
	Subtraction	Practical work with tens and units (involving decomposition)	Subtraction of tens and units (with decomposition)	Subtraction of hundreds, tens and units (with decomposition)
	Multiplication		Repeated addition. Compilation of tables 2, 5, 10	Compilation of tables: 3, 4, 6, 7, 8, 9. Multiplication of tens and units by single integer and 10
	Division		Practical sharing of tens and units involving decomposition (MAB materials), involving remainders	Division of tens and units involving decomposition and remainders
	Money		Equivalence, addition and subtraction up to £1	Calculating change from £1. Application. Decimal notation
	Fractions		Equivalence of $\frac{1}{2}$ and $\frac{1}{4}$	Equivalence of $\frac{1}{4}$, $\frac{1}{2}$, $\frac{3}{4}$ and whole one
	Decimals			
	Percentages			
	Patterns and Relationships	Number line work. Odds and evens	Odds and evens. Table patterns. Calculator problems. Consecutive numbers	Function machines. Digit patterns. Number patterns. Equations
MEASURES	Length	Measuring in cm with metre stick	Measuring in cm with ruler. Measuring with variety of tools	Equivalence of m and cm. Measuring diameters. Reading numbers on instruments
	Weight	Weighing with kilogram weight (greater than, less than, equal to)	Balancing with grams	Equivalence of kg and g. Estimating and weighing in g. Reading numbers on instruments
	Capacity	Measuring capacity with litre jug (greater than, less than, equal to)	Estimation/measuring of a litre. Use of millilitre and litre	Estimating and measuring in ml. Reading numbers on instruments
	Area			
	Volume			
	Time		Minutes past notation (digital recording). Calendar	Relative times: minutes past notation
SHAPE AND SPACE		Square corners: three- and four-sided shapes	Names of plane and solid shapes. Tessellation. Symmetry	Vertices, faces. Diagonals. Tetrahedron. Patterns. Polygons. Geoboard work. Turning $\frac{1}{4}$, $\frac{1}{2}$, turns. Clockwise, anti-clockwise
HANDLING DATA			Column graph (1 : 1). Venn diagram. Stick graph (involving scale)	Column graph (1 : 2). Recording in matrix form. Tables. Chance using dice

Peak Four	Peak Extra		
Rounding off; large numbers Approximation ($\simeq$); number systems Using, applying and consolidating	Index notation; number bases. Approximations Using, applying and consolidating	**Notation**	**NUMBER AND ALGEBRA**
Using, applying and consolidating	Using, applying and consolidating	**Addition**	
Using, applying and consolidating	Using, applying and consolidating	**Subtraction**	
Using, applying and consolidating Factors	Using, applying and consolidating	**Multiplication**	
Using, applying and consolidating Factors	Using, applying and consolidating	**Division**	
Using, applying and consolidating	Using, applying and consolidating	**Money**	
Fractions of areas, distances, volumes, angles Equivalence work Fractions of amounts	Continuous halving General fraction work	**Fractions**	
Equivalence of fractions and decimals Rounding off Using, applying and consolidating	Approximation Using, applying and consolidating	**Decimals**	
Finding percentages of number and money Discount, interest	Discount Bank accounts Using, applying and consolidating	**Percentages**	
Number patterns. Prime numbers Calculator problems Co-ordinates Equations Number systems	Brackets, inverse operations, functions Mappings. Square roots, number patterns Simple equations. Graphing equations	**Patterns and Relationships**	
Map work, scales Practical measurement of diameters and circumferences Heights of tall buildings Imperial units	Circumference of circles (π) Imperial units Using, applying and consolidating	**Length**	**MEASURES**
Reading of scales Imperial units Using, applying and consolidating	Imperial units Using, applying and consolidating	**Weight**	
Reading scales Using, applying and consolidating	Imperial units Using, applying and consolidating	**Capacity**	
Halving areas Areas of right-angled triangles Approximate area of a circle	Areas of irregular shapes Areas of circles Surface area	**Area**	
Volume of a cuboid Displacement activities Halving volumes	Volume of cylinders Using, applying and consolidating	**Volume**	
Sunrise/sunset (24 hour clock) Pendulum Using, applying and consolidating	Using, applying and consolidating	**Time**	
Parallelogram, trapezium, rhombus Rotational symmetry, patterns Cardioid Stars, spirals, tetrahedron Construction of shapes; protractors Clinometer Angles of elevation	Constructions. Enlargements. Nets. Rigidity. Ellipse. Truncated tetrahedron, symmetries, Patterns. Reflex angles (360° protractor) Bearings	**SHAPE AND SPACE**	
Wide range of data handling, collecting, drawing and interpretation. Map work Probability	Wide range of data handling: collecting, drawing and interpretation Probability, likelihood	**HANDLING DATA**	

Peak Two part 1	Peak Two part 2	Peak Three
Fractions on number lines Abacus Digit values	Using, applying and consolidating Reading, writing and ordering numbers	Using, applying and consolidating Multiplying and dividing by 10 and multiples of 10
Addition over 1000	Addition of thousands, hundreds, tens and units Using, applying and consolidating	Using, applying and consolidating
Subtraction of hundreds, tens and units (with decomposition) Difference (various formats)	Subtraction of thousands, hundreds, tens and units Using, applying and consolidating	Using, applying and consolidating
Multiplication of hundreds, tens and units by single integer and 10	Multiplication of hundreds, tens and units Using, applying and consolidating	Using, applying and consolidating Multiples, products
Division of hundreds, tens and units Fractions of quantities	Division of thousands, hundreds, tens and units Remainders Factors Using, applying and consolidating	Using, applying and consolidating Average
Application involving addition, subtraction and multiplication	Using, applying and consolidating Combination of coins	Using, applying and consolidating
Fractions of quantities Halving numbers with a calculator	Equivalences of: $\frac{1}{2}, \frac{1}{4}, \frac{1}{8}, \frac{1}{5}, \frac{1}{10}$	General equivalence of fractions Mixed numbers
	Decimal numbers (one place of decimals) Notation in measures	Decimal numbers (two places of decimals)
Consecutive numbers Magic squares Number patterns Odds and evens	Square numbers Calculator problems Number patterns	Triangular numbers. Brackets Calculator problems. Prime numbers Roman numbers Co-ordinates
Perimeter: using and applying involving m and cm Estimating	Perimeter Metre notation Using, applying and consolidating	Use of km and mm: estimating Plans and scales Using, applying and consolidating
Comparison of weights: various items and substances Reading off calibrated scales	Kilogram notation Using, applying and consolidating	Equivalence of kg and g: estimating Reading calibrated scales/balances Using, applying and consolidating
Finding weight of litres of various substances	Litre notation Using, applying and consolidating	Equivalence of l and ml: estimating Using, applying and consolidating
Finding area by counting squares and half squares	Area in cm²	Areas of rectangles and composite shapes. Geoboard work. Square metre
		Volume of cuboids Use of cm³
am and pm Making timers Calendar	Reading of television timetable Using, applying and consolidating	Seconds (stopwatch) 24 hour clock Calendar Using, applying and consolidating
Line symmetry Tessellating patterns Four points of the compass Right angle Set square	Pentominoes. Nets. Symmetry in quadrilaterals Angles in shapes Right angle shapes Half right angles	Paper folding. Symmetry Diameter, radius, circumference. Compass work. Tangrams. Isosceles triangle Angle properties of polygons Protractor work Acute/obtuse angles Totals of angles in triangles and quadrilaterals
Column graph (1 : 10) Time tables Calendars	Timetables Column graphs Weather charts	Co-ordinates Charts Stick graphs Map work Line graphs Time tables Conversion tables

Photocopy

National Curriculum references for New Peak Two materials

Details of the Attainment Targets, at the various levels, covered by the *New Peak Two* pupils materials, are shown below.

This book also contains suggestions for a rich variety of activities across all the Attainment Targets.

New Peak Two part 1

Attainment Targets	Level 3	Level 4
1	▓	
2	▓	▓
3	▓	
4	▓	
5	▓	

New Peak Two part 2

Attainment Targets	Level 4	
1	▓	
2	▓	
3	▓	
4	▓	
5	▓	

Peak Explorer Two part 1

Attainment Targets	Level 3	Level 4
1	▓	▓
2	▓	▓
3		▓
4		▓

Peak Explorer Two part 2

Attainment Targets	Level 3	Level 4
1	▓	▓
2	▓	
3		
4	▓	

New Peak Two Plus

Attainment Targets	Level 3	Level 4
1	▓	▓
2	▓	
3	▓	
4	▓	
5	▓	

Number Skills Two

Attainment Targets	Level 3	Level 4
2	▓	▓
3	▓	

For a more detailed analysis of the Peak core materials in relation to the National Curriculum, please refer to the *Peak Mathematics and the National Curriculum Correlations* document available free of charge from the publishers.

Testing

Mathematics testing in school takes many different forms. It is important that thought is given to the specific purpose of the tests and their content. Much testing is ongoing and done incidentally by teachers; indeed, with a structured approach to mathematics, each time a child applies acquired skills to a new situation, his or her expertise is being tested. However, in more formal situations, whether it be a class test set by the teacher or a commercial test, it is sensible to consider the content in some detail, to ensure that the purpose of the test is clear.

Before looking directly at actual test content, it would perhaps be helpful to consider the structured development built into the Peak materials. Throughout the scheme, for each new skill area to which they are introduced, the children are given:

1 practical experience which develops understanding of the process and language involved and leads to
2 the abstraction and practice of computational skills, which lead to
3 the application of the experience gained and the skills acquired to a new mathematical situation.

These stages also apply to testing. The questions within tests can be summarised into four categories as follows:

1 questions to test understanding of processes (place value, decomposition, finding area, etc.)
2 questions to test computational skills (oral, written, calculator)
3 questions to test factual recall (names of shapes, etc.)
4 questions to test ability to apply skills to new problems.

The assessment tests built into the Peak materials concentrate largely on categories 1, 2 and 3 in order to show whether the skills and language developed in each book are sufficiently well established for further development and application. A child's ability to apply acquired skills (category 4) will be continuously tested by the content of subsequent books.

Tests prepared by teachers for their own use should ideally contain questions in all the four categories, unless they are specifically intended to test one particular area (e.g. a tables test).

Standardised tests are available for 7 to 12 year olds which, as well as giving individual scores, show a child's performance in each of the categories of question outlined above. These are marketed by NFER Nelson and are called *Mathematics 7 to 12*.

Classroom organisation

The range of activities within **peak mathematics** include:
- concept building activities
- skill development activities
- word problems
- real problems
- open-ended tasks
- opportunities for the use of a wide range of materials
- oral/mental activities
- calculator activities
- games
- puzzles
- opportunities for extended pieces of work

Whilst the materials allow individual teachers and schools to decide on classroom organisation, it will be seen from the types of activity listed above that at different times the children will work on:

1 class based activities
2 corporate group activities
3 individualised activities

Whatever the organisation, children should not be allowed to meet concepts, skills and processes which have not been taught, otherwise they may experience repeated failure.

Focus of Pupils' Books Peak Two part 1 and Peak Two part 2

The following areas of development in the Pupils' Books require considerable support from the teacher.

Peak Two part 1

Place value
Equivalence of thousands, hundreds, tens and units

Addition of thousands, hundreds, tens and units

Subtraction of hundreds, tens and units by decomposition
Difference aspect of subtraction

Multiplication tables
Multiplication of two- and three-digit numbers

Division within table facts
Division of hundreds, tens and units
Fractional aspect of division

Equivalence involving quarters

Equivalence of centimetres and metres

Ability to read dials and scales on measuring instruments

Counting partial squares when finding area

Peak Two part 2

Quick methods of computation

Square numbers

Factors

Notation used in length (4·50 m)
Notation used in weight (1·250 kg)
Notation used in capacity (2·750 l)
Notation used in area (24 cm²)

Equivalence of eighth family
Equivalence of tenth family

Decimal numbers (to one place of decimals)

Simple time calculations (between times which go over the hour)

Number and Algebra

The Number and Algebra work developed in these modules is based on four main areas:

- **number values**   whole, fractional and decimal numbers
- **number operations**   addition, subtraction, multiplication and division
- **number relationships**   commutativity, number trios, associativity
- **number patterns**   square numbers, consecutive numbers, odds and evens

During the course of this development, the children should be involved in mental and oral activities, written work, and work with the calculator. The format of presentation includes puzzles, games, investigations, word problems and problem solving.

It is important not to neglect activities involving numbers less than 20 even though the focus may be on operations with larger numbers.

Addition

Whilst the children are working on the addition modules in *Peak Two* (parts 1 and 2) they will have experience of activities which:

- develop and extend their knowledge of number bonds
- introduce and develop addition of larger numbers (using place value concepts)
- encourage the use of quick mental calculations
- help them to recognise the result of adding odd and even numbers.

During the activities the children should become more proficient at number bond recall, should develop the ability to add numbers where exchange between columns is required, and should discover more informal methods of addition.

Number bond and small number activities

These activities may be interspersed with the addition modules as appropriate. Because they are mainly concerned with number bond relationships, they may also be used within other Number modules, such as subtraction.

**Number Skills Two
Peak Explorer Two
(parts 1 and 2)**

These books offer further pupil material involving the processes, skills and language associated with addition.

Peak Plus

The following pages from *Peak Plus 2* may be appropriate for children looking at number bonds during the addition modules.

Number links   page 6
Joined pairs   page 20
Number stories   page 22
Tractor paths   page 25
Number neighbours   page 32
Make a hundred   page 33

Mirror numbers

'Draw 10 circles on a card.
Can a mirror be placed on the card to show 12 circles?
Can a mirror be placed on the card to show each number from 1 to 20?'

(Odd numbers are formed by placing a mirror across a circle.)

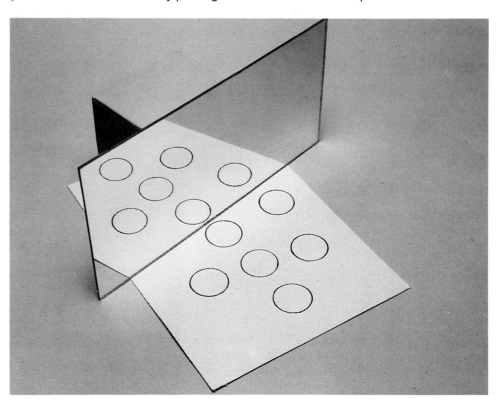

Balancing washers
The children use four washers and a number balance.
All four washers must be placed on the balance.
The same numbers cannot be used each side, for example, 3 and 1 balanced by 3 and 1.
Sides cannot be 'mirrored', for example, 5 and 5 with 9 and 1 is the same as 9 and 1 with 5 and 5.
More than one washer is allowed on each number.

Odds
The washers can only be placed on odd numbers.

'Will two washers balance two washers?'

'How many different ways can you find?'
(There are seven different ways:

1 and 5 with 3 and 3	1 and 9 with 5 and 5
1 and 7 with 3 and 5	3 and 9 with 5 and 7
1 and 9 with 3 and 7	5 and 9 with 7 and 7.)
3 and 7 with 5 and 5	

'Will three washers balance one washer?'

'How many ways can you find?'
(There are seven different ways:

1, 1, 1 with 3	1, 3, 3 with 7
1, 1, 3 with 5	1, 3, 5 with 9
1, 1, 5 with 7	3, 3, 3 with 9.)
1, 1, 7 with 9	

Change the rule so that only odd numbers are allowed on the left hand side of the balance and only even numbers on the right.
The children can now experiment to make the washers balance.
Note that in this instance three washers will not balance one washer.

Domino squares   The children make domino squares where every side is an odd number. 'How many separate squares can you make?'

The children make domino squares where every side is a square number. 'How many separate squares can you make?'

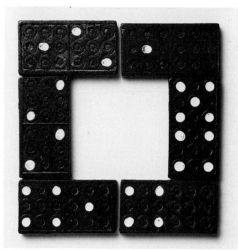

L numbers   Odd numbers make L-shapes.

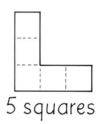 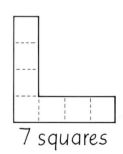

I square

3 squares

5 squares

7 squares

If L numbers are put together they make square numbers.

 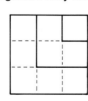

$1 + 3 = 4$

$1 + 3 + 5 = 9$

This shows that square numbers can be made by adding consecutive odd numbers.

Number chains   The children choose a simple set of rules, for example:
If a number is even, halve it.
If a number is odd, add 11.

They choose a starting number, for example 14.

They now apply the rules:
14 – even, so halve it to get 7
7 – odd, so add 11 to get 18
18 – even, so halve it to get 9
and so on.

Starting with 14, a chain is made which comes back to the starting number.

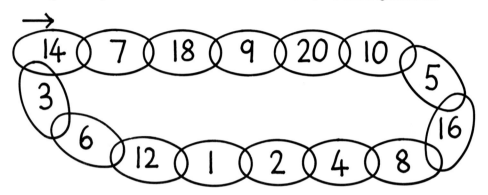

The children should try other starting numbers.
Will the chains always return to the start?
How many links in each chain?

Numeral cards   The children choose any four numeral cards.

$$\boxed{6} \quad \boxed{1} \quad \boxed{4} \quad \boxed{7}$$

Which numbers up to 20 can be made by addition?

$$\boxed{6} + \boxed{1} = 7 \qquad \boxed{6} + \boxed{4} = 10 \qquad \boxed{6} + \boxed{1} + \boxed{7} = 14$$

Which set of numeral cards will make all the numbers up to 20?
(One possible answer is 1, 2, 4, 8, 9.)

Dice totals   A game for two players.

Each player rolls two dice in turn.
A score is obtained by finding the total of:
the numbers added $5 + 2 = 7$
the difference between the numbers and $5 - 2 = 3$
the numbers multiplied. $5 \times 2 = 10$
                                                                        $\overline{20}$

The winner is the first to reach 200.

Additions with larger numbers

Peak Plus The following pages from *Peak Plus 2* may be appropriate for children working on the addition modules.

Peak Posters The following posters can produce some interesting work with additions:

Calculator lights
Darts scores
Digit grid
Domino squares

Forbidden keys The children use a calculator.

It is forbidden to touch a nominated key (for example, 6). Challenge the children to find different ways of using the calculator to solve additions which include the 'forbidden' digit.

56	64	366	165
+59	+56	+274	+666

Mental adds Children with a good number bond facility should be encouraged to extend this to larger numbers through mental activities. Some children find that answering with their eyes shut helps. Others find imagining a number line in their mind and moving along that line helpful.

'Make these numbers up to the next hundred.
What must be added?
63 37 12 137 448 213 309'

'Eyes closed.
Think of 146.
Add on 20.
Add on 8.
What is the new number?'

'The answer is 145.
Which two 2-digit numbers could have been added together?'

Consecutives   'Three consecutive numbers have been added together.
Here are the answers.
What were the numbers?
You can use a calculator if you want to.'

57 (Answer: 18 + 19 + 20)   105 (Answer: 34 + 35 + 36)

156 (Answer: 51 + 52 + 53)   204 (Answer: 67 + 68 + 69)

Codes   Addition sums can be decoded to produce a word.
This is an exercise which is self checking.

```
Code
A E R S T
2 6 9 1 8

  S E T
+ S A T
_____

_____

Find the word your
answer makes
```

```
Code
T A E P C M
0 7 4 3 1 5

  P A T
+ C A T
_____

_____

Find the word your
answer makes
```

Estimation   Calculators can be used to give practice in estimating answers.
Give the children a series of additions and ask them to ring the best estimate.
They then check with the calculator.

Sum	Estimate			Answer
25 + 46	50	60	70	
32 + 59	70	80	90	
64 + 33	100	110	120	
50 + 54	100	110	120	
99 + 89	140	160	190	

Calculator words

Calculator displays can be used to make words when turned upside down.

710 becomes OIL

733 becomes EEL

The children could make up additions which give calculator words. For example, 220 + 443 produces EGG when displayed upside down.

Domino sums

The children use dominoes to make addition sums.

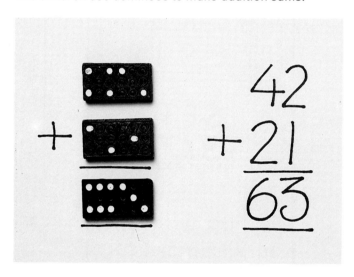

$$
\begin{array}{r}
42 \\
+\ 21 \\
\hline
63
\end{array}
$$

Making up

This can be done by counting on.

Make up to 500	Make up to 1000
374 →	329 →
156 →	560 →
89 →	437 →
406 →	904 →
72 →	385 →

Subtraction

Whilst the children are working on the subtraction modules in *Peak Two* (parts 1 and 2) they will have experience of activities which:

● develop and extend their knowledge of number bonds
● develop the subtraction of larger numbers by decomposition
● extend ideas of 'difference'.

During the activities the children should become more proficient at number bond recall, should develop the ability to subtract numbers where exchange between columns is required, and should discover more informal methods of subtraction (quick methods).

The activities include the different subtraction situations 'taking away', 'difference' and 'complementary addition'.

Number bond and small number activities

These activities may be interspersed with the activities in the subtraction modules as appropriate. Because they are mainly concerned with number bond relationships, they may also be used within other Number modules such as addition.

**Number Skills Two
Peak Explorer Two
(parts 1 and 2)**

These books offer further pupil material involving the processes, skills and language associated with subtraction.

Peak Plus

The following page from *Peak Plus 2* may be appropriate for children looking at number bonds during the subtraction modules.

Number links page 6

Six touch

The only keys which may be touched are:

7 3 − + =

The calculator can only be touched *six* times.
Which answers can be obtained?

 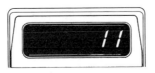  

Target

The target is 21.

Only $\boxed{5}$ $\boxed{4}$ $\boxed{\times}$ $\boxed{-}$ $\boxed{=}$ can be used.

The children find different ways of reaching the target (for example, $5 - 4 \times 5 \times 5 - 4 = 21$)

What is the smallest number of touches to reach the target?

Can the target be reached in 12 touches? Change the target number.

Numeral cards

The children choose four different numeral cards. $\boxed{9}$ $\boxed{4}$ $\boxed{2}$ $\boxed{1}$

How many different answers can be made by finding differences?

$\boxed{9} - \boxed{1} = 8$ $\boxed{4} - \boxed{2} = 2$ $\boxed{1}\boxed{4} - \boxed{2} = 12$

Number triangles

Make triangles with missing numbers at the vertices.
The children have to put a number at each vertex so that the side numbers are the differences.
There are many different correct answers.

Restrictions can be imposed such as only using odd numbers.

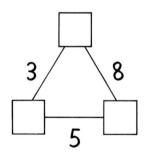

Find the difference

'Arrange the digits 1 to 9 in the boxes.
Write the differences between adjacent boxes on the lines.
Total the differences.
Find the smallest total possible.'

A calculator may be useful.
Digit cards can be used in the activity to allow the digits to be rearranged.

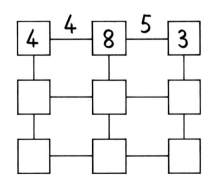

Subtractions with larger numbers

Peak Plus The following pages from *Peak Plus 2* may be appropriate for children who are investigating subtraction of larger numbers.

Dice game	page 10
Spike abacus	page 15
Calculator quickies	page 26
Making answers	page 43

Magic columns The child subtracts any number in the second column from any number in the first column. He or she then adds the digits of the answer and continues to do so until a single digit is obtained.

e.g.

$$\begin{array}{r} 441 \\ -\ 151 \\ \hline 290 \\ \hline \end{array} \qquad \begin{array}{r} 360 \\ -\ 205 \\ \hline 155 \\ \hline \end{array} \qquad \begin{array}{r} 702 \\ -\ 106 \\ \hline 596 \\ \hline \end{array}$$

$2 + 9 + 0 = 11$ $1 + 5 + 5 = 11$ $5 + 9 + 6 = 20$
$1 + 1 = 2$ $1 + 1 = 2$ $2 + 0 = 2$

(The final answer will remain constant so long as the digits in each number in the first column add up to a constant number, and similarly for the second column. The same activity can be used for addition.)

441	106
360	205
702	61
414	151
801	43

The digits of each number add up to 9.

The digits of each number add up to 7.

Domino subtractions The children use dominoes to make subtractions.

$$\begin{array}{r} 61 \\ -\ 36 \\ \hline 25 \\ \hline \end{array}$$

Reduce to zero 'Make 5 subtractions which will give an answer of zero at the end.

Check your subtraction chain with a calculator.'

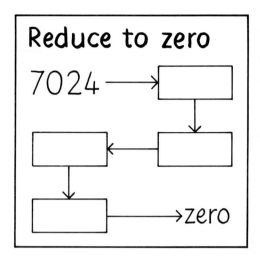

What is the question? The child has to make up questions to fit the answers.

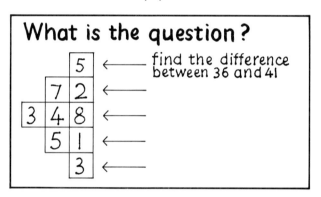

Missing numbers The children fill in missing digits where the operation is either an addition or a subtraction.

Even though the sign suggests it is an addition operation, it may be necessary to subtract in order to find the solution.

```
    37          **          48          **
  + **        + 34        - **        - 29
  ____        ____        ____        ____
    91          72          19          58
  ____        ____        ____        ____
```

Forbidden keys The children use a calculator.
It is forbidden to touch a nominated key (for example, 6).
Challenge the children to find different ways of using the calculator to solve subtractions which include the 'forbidden' digit.

```
    76          64         366         965
  - 49        - 56       - 294       - 566
  ____        ____       _____       _____

  ____        ____       _____       _____
```

Mental subtractions   Children with a good number bond facility should be encouraged to extend this to larger numbers through mental activities.
Some children find that answering with their eyes shut helps. Others find imagining a number line in their mind and moving back along that line helpful.

'Subtract these numbers from 200.
152 174 157 73 95'

'Eyes closed.
Think of 96.
Subtract 40.
Subtract 8.
What is the new number?'

'The difference is 35.
Which two 2-digit numbers could have this difference?'

Calculator words   Calculator displays can be used to make words when turned upside down.

7334 becomes HEEL

The children could make up subtractions which give calculator words.
For example, 1000 − 229 produces ILL when displayed upside down.

Multiplication

Whilst the children are working on the multiplication modules in *Peak Two* (parts 1 and 2) they will have experience of activities which:

- develop and extend their knowledge of multiplication bonds
- develop their ability to multiply larger numbers
- encourage the use of informal methods of multiplication
- introduce square numbers
- develop their knowledge of the commutative property of multiplication.

The notation used throughout the modules is that 3×4 means $3 + 3 + 3 + 3$ rather than $4 + 4 + 4$.

The table facts which cause particular difficulty are:
8×6, 7×9, 8×7, 4×9, 9×6, 8×8, 7×6, 8×4, 7×7, 9×4
The children may need extra practice with these facts.

Multiplication bond activities

Number Skills Two
Peak Explorer Two
(parts 1 and 2)

These books offer further pupil material involving the processes, skills and language associated with multiplication.

Peak Plus

The following pages from *Peak Plus 2* may be appropriate for children investigating multiplication.

Make a hundred page 33
Calculator quest page 47

Triangle flash cards

Table facts are written on triangular cards.
One of the corners is covered with the thumb or the fingers.
Ask which number is 'hidden'.
The children can play this in pairs, each hiding a number in turn.

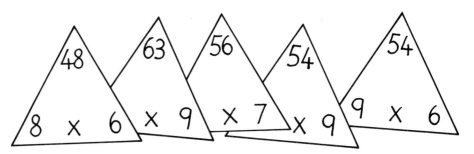

Domino squares

The children make domino squares where every side is a multiple of 5.

They can also make domino squares with sides which are a multiple of other numbers.

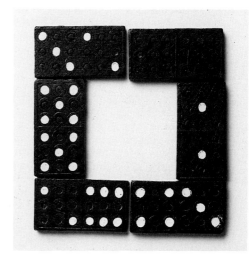

Multiplication square shapes

The children can make different shapes by colouring in even numbers on a multiplication square.

a plus sign

a boat

1	2	3	4	5	6	7	8	9	10
2	4	6	8	10	12	14	16	18	20
3	6	9	12	15	18	21	24	27	30
4	8	12	16	20	24	28	32	36	40
5	10	15	20	25	30	35	40	45	50
6	12	18	24	30	36	42	48	54	60
7	14	21	28	35	42	49	56	63	70
8	16	24	32	40	48	56	64	72	80
9	18	27	36	45	54	63	72	81	90
10	20	30	40	50	60	70	80	90	100

a hollow square

Which capital letters can be made by colouring even numbers?

4	6	8
6	9	12
8	12	16
10	15	20

letter A

48	54	60
56	63	70
64	72	80
72	81	90
80	90	100

letter B

18	21	24
24	28	32
30	35	40

letter H

Snakes alive

An 'empty' snake is drawn.
One child starts off by writing a simple number statement such as 5 × 4.
The next child's statement must begin with the answer to the previous one, for example, 20 ÷ 2.
The activity continues in this way.
Constraints can be placed on the activity, for example, no answer can exceed 50; no odd answers.

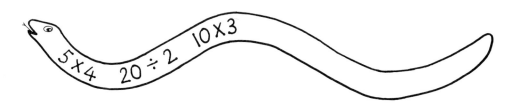

Multiple patience

The children use playing cards without the picture cards.
They place four cards face up.
The rest of the pack stays face down.
One card at a time is turned over from the pack. This card can be placed below any of the cards which are face up.
When a column adds up to a multiple of 10, it can be removed.
Can all the columns be removed before the pack runs out?

The third column can be removed as it adds up to 20.

Multiple grids

A game for two or more players.

Each child has a grid of numbers which are multiples of 4.
The children roll two dice in turn.
The total on the dice is multiplied by 4 and the appropriate number on the grid is covered with a counter.
The first to cover the grid is the winner.

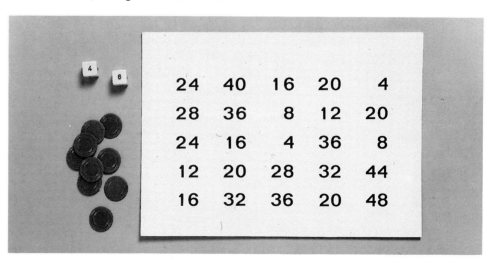

Grids with multiples of other numbers can also be used.

Triangle grids The children roll two dice.
They use any operation ($+ - \times \div$).
How many rolls of the dice to cover the triangle?

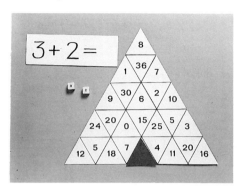

Table answers The children find out how many different answers they have to remember when learning their tables (up to 10 $\times$ 10).
There are remarkably few answers!

```
100
 90
 80  81
 70  72
 60  63  64
 50  54  56
 40  42  45  48  49
 30  32  35  36
 20  21  24  25  27  28
 10  12  14  15  16  18
  2   3   4   5   6   7   8   9
```

Ask questions like:
'The answer is 81. What could the question be?'
'The answer is 54. What could the question be?'
'Which tables contain the answer 36?'
'Which tables contain the answer 81?'

Rod cubes 'Build a cube with 2-rods.
Use as few rods as possible.
How many rods are needed?'

Repeat with rods of other sizes.

The number of rods needed gives the square number sequence.

Rods used	Number to make a cube
2-rods	4
3-rods	9
4-rods	16
5-rods	25
etc.	

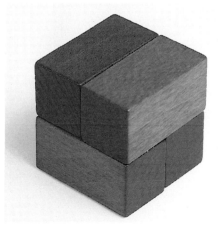

Multiplications with larger numbers

Changing numbers   Using a calculator, the children change from one given number to another by multiplying and dividing only.
If a decimal number appears in the display, they must go back to the beginning.

For example, change 6 to 400.

| × 100 | ÷ 3 | × 2 |

Consecutive numbers   The children use a calculator to find which consecutive numbers multiplied together produce the answers.

* × * × * = 504
(Answer: 7 × 8 × 9)

* × * × * = 210
(Answer: 5 × 6 × 7)

* × * × * = 120
(Answer: 4 × 5 × 6)

* × * × * = 720
(Answer: 8 × 9 × 10)

Rod abacus   The children use an abacus with three rods and four beads.
Which square numbers can be made?

They could try with five beads, six beads, and so on.
A calculator can be used to check.

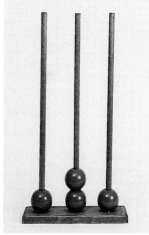

Beads	Square numbers on three rods
4	4, 121, 400
5	none
6	none
7	16, 25
8	none
9	9, 36, 81, 144, 225, 324, 441, 900

Three digit puzzle   Write any 3-digit number where the first digit is the smallest and the last the largest

278

1 Take the hundreds digit and double it.   4
2 Add 20.   24
3 Multiply by 5.   120
4 Add the tens digit of the starting number.   127
5 Multiply by 10.   1270
6 Add the unit digit of the starting number.   1278
7 Subtract 1000.   278

Will it work with other numbers?

Ton up Which digits can be made into 100 by multiplication only?
For example, 2 ($\times$ 5 $\times$ 10) = 100
3 (cannot be done)
4 ($\times$ 5 $\times$ 5) = 100

Which can be made into 200, 300 and so on?
(Those which can be made into 100 can be made into any multiple of 100.)

Forbidden key The 7 key on the calculator may not be touched.
Find different ways of solving these:

23 $\times$ 7   74 $\times$ 5   77 $\times$ 8   27 $\times$ 27

Decade times The children should practise multiplying decade numbers by single digits.

40 $\times$ 6   60 $\times$ 9   30 $\times$ 5   50 $\times$ 6   90 $\times$ 8   and so on.

This can be a mental activity.

The children could break the decade number into a multiple of 10 before
multiplying: 40 $\times$ 4 = 4 $\times$ 10 $\times$ 4.
They could also experiment with breaking the decade number into other component
factors:

$$40 \times 4 = 8 \times 5 \times 4$$
$$= 2 \times 4 \times 5 \times 4$$
$$= 2 \times 2 \times 2 \times 5 \times 2 \times 2$$

Into memory Encourage the children to try to multiply two-digit and one-digit numbers in their
heads. A 'put it into memory' technique can help with this process. For example:

24 $\times$ 7
20 $\times$ 7 = 140   Close your eyes and put 140 into memory.
4 $\times$ 7 = 28   Add 28 to the number in your memory.

Division

Whilst the children are working on the division modules in *Peak Two* (parts 1 and 2) they will have experience of activities which:

● develop and extend their knowledge of division bonds
● develop their ability to divide larger numbers
● introduce factors.

The activities show division as:

● sharing a quantity into a given number of equal groups
● sharing into groups of stated quantity (repeated subtraction).

The language and 'patter' which develop out of these two division situations are very different.

A relationship should be shown between multiplication and division bonds. For example:

$3 \times 4 = 12$ $4 \times 3 = 12$
$12 \div 4 = 3$ $12 \div 3 = 4$

The remainders which arise in some division problems are dealt with in these modules.

The children will use several notations to show division, for example:

$56 \div 8$ $8\overline{)56}$ $\dfrac{56}{8}$

The children will be involved in the division of two- and three-digit numbers where some exchanging will occur.

Division bond activities

Number Skills Two
Peak Explorer Two
(parts 1 and 2)

These books offer further pupil material involving the processes, skills and language associated with division.

Peak Plus

The following pages from *Peak Plus 2* may be appropriate for children investigating division.

Rectangles and rods   page 14
Number tracks   page 39
Rod pairs   page 42

Remainders

A number of counters is put out, say 27.
'How many 4s in 27?'
'What is the remainder?'

'How many 5s in 27?'
'What is the remainder?'

'Which divisions give a zero remainder?'
'Which divisions give two as a remainder?'
and so on.

Equal sets   Focus upon a number and share it into equal sets.
For example, 18 counters:
'Shared into 2 equal groups, any remainder?'
'Shared into 3 equal groups, any remainder?'
'Shared into 4 equal groups, any remainder?'

'Which leave no remainders?'

Line jumps   '32 can be reached in 4 equal jumps.
Which other equal jumps will reach 32?'

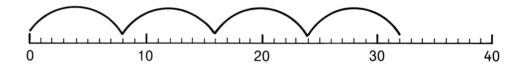

'Which equal jumps will reach 28?'

The children could try with other target numbers.

Rods   'How many 3-rods will match 15?'
'How many 5-rods will match 15?'
This activity develops early ideas on
factors.

'How many 2-rods will match 16?'
'Say how many 8-rods. Were you right?'
'Which other rods will match it?'

Focus on remainders

'The remainder is 7.
What could I have divided by?'
(Answer: any number greater than seven.)

'The remainder is 3.'
'What could the question have been?'
(Answer: 15 ÷ 4, 27 ÷ 8, etc.)

'I am thinking of a number.
I divide it by 5.
The remainder is 2.
What could the number have been?'
(Answer: 7, 12, 17, 22, etc.)

Cards

A game for two players.

Use a pack of playing cards without the pictures.
The players take turns to remove two cards from the top of the pack.
A two-digit number is made from the cards.
The player lists all the known factors of that number and then totals them.
One and the number itself are not allowed.

The winner can be either the first player to pass a nominated target or the one with the greatest total when all the cards have been exhausted.

Disagreements can be resolved by using a calculator to check whether a certain number is a factor.

Division with larger numbers

Rod abacus

The children use an abacus with three rods and three beads.
All the beads must be used each time.
They make numbers which are exactly divisible by 3.
Can a number be made which is not divisible by 3?
(Every number made with three beads will be divisible by three.)

Can numbers be made which are divisible by four, five, six, etc.?
(It is impossible to make a number which is divisible by nine.)

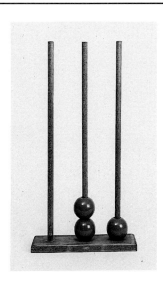

Nines The children use an abacus with three rods and several beads.
They make numbers which are divisible by nine.
How many beads are needed for each number?

(Nine beads, or a multiple of nine, will always be needed.)

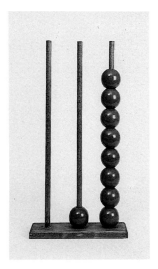

Any remainder? Write any 4-digit number.   4712
Rearrange the digits in any way.   2741

Subtract the smaller from the larger.   1971
Divide the answer by 9.

Is there a remainder?   219
                                                9) 1971

Repeat this a number of times.
(There will never be a remainder.)

Other ways

'You are not allowed to divide by 6.
Find ways of solving the problem.'

For example, $90 \div 3 \div 2$; $45 \div 3$

'You are not allowed to divide by 12.
Find ways of solving the problem.'

For example, $216 \div 6 \div 2$; $216 \div 3 \div 4$; $108 \div 6$; $54 \div 3$

Fractions

Whilst the children are working on the fraction modules in *Peak Two* (parts 1 and 2) they will have experience of activities which:

● develop and extend the concept of fractions
● develop the concept of equivalent fractions.

The activities show:

fractions of a shape

fractions of a composite shape

fractions of a quantitiy

fractions as a position on a number line

The division aspect of fractions (for example, $\frac{36}{9}$) is dealt with in the division modules.

Peak Explorer Two (parts 1 and 2) These books offer further pupil material involving the processes, skills and language associated with fractions.

Peak Plus The following pages from *Peak Plus 2* may be appropriate for children investigating early ideas of fractions.

Peak Posters   The Peak Poster 'Halving Squares' provides a useful starting point for an investigation of fractions of a shape.

Class Topic   On page 90 of this book there are suggestions for topic work on fractions which involves a whole class or group of children.

Fractions of shapes   'Colour $\frac{1}{4}$ of the squares to make a symmetrical pattern.
Colour $\frac{1}{2}$ of the squares to make a symmetrical pattern.
Now colour $\frac{3}{4}$ of the squares to make a symmetrical pattern.'

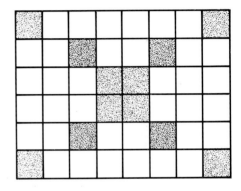

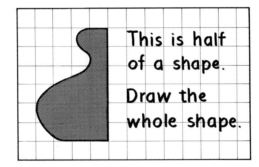

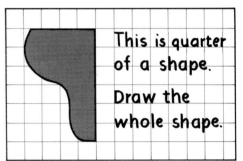

'Cut this shape from squared paper.
Cut it in half.
How many different new shapes can be made by putting the two halves together?'

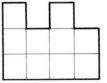

For example, cutting in half like this:

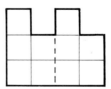

can give these shapes and many others.

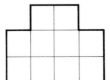 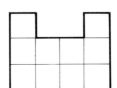 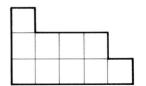

'This is half a shape.
Cut two out of squared paper.
How many different whole shapes can
be made?'

Possible whole shapes include:

How many different ways can this shape
be halved?

Possible solutions include:

Similar work can be done with quarters and three-quarters of various shapes.

Fractions on a geoboard

The children can find a half and a quarter of a 9-pin geoboard.
This can be extended to include eighths (and multiples of eighths) on a 9-pin board.
Similar work can be done on boards of other sizes. The children can find out which fractions cannot be made in this way on certain boards.

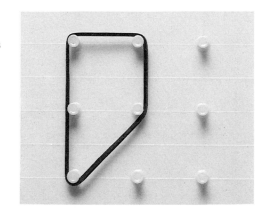

Similar work to the above can be done on a rectangular geoboard (for example, 3 × 4). Such a board can be made from a 4 × 4 board by 'blanking off' one row of pins with an elastic band.

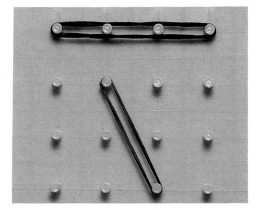

How many ways can a 3 × 4 board be halved?
1 using neither middle pin?
2 using one middle pin only?
3 using both middle pins?
Similar work can be done with other fractions.

The children find as many ways as they can to 'chop off' 2 squares.

The children find ways of dividing the 3 × 4 board into thirds.

In all these activities with geoboards, recording can be done on spotty paper.

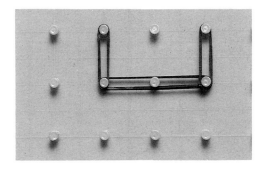

Paper folding

'Use a plain strip of paper.
Mark where you think $\frac{1}{2}$ of the strip is.
Fold the paper to check how accurate
you were.'

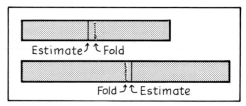

'Fold a piece of paper in half, then fold again, then again. Colour the side facing you.
What fraction of the paper has been coloured?
Open the paper out to check.'

The child could be asked to fold the paper twice and colour only a half of the side facing him or her.
'What fraction has been coloured?'

Equivalence of number rods

'Which of these rods can be matched with 2-rods?'
The children investigate the matching of rods.

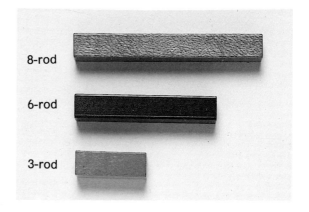

The results could be tabulated.

Rod	Can be matched with
2-rod	1-rods
3-rod	1-rods
4-rod	1-rods, 2-rods
5-rod	1-rods
6-rod	1-rods, 2-rods, 3-rods

Decimals

Whilst the children are working on the decimal module in *Peak Two* (part 2) they will have experience of activities which:

● introduce decimal notation to one place of decimals.

Within the **peak mathematics** scheme, the decimal point is used in two ways:
1 as a *separator* in measurement notation and money notation (for example, 5·25 m, 1·500 kg, 4·250 l, £3·70). It separates the metres from the centimetres, the pounds from the pennies, and so on.
2 as a *marker* between units and tenths in number notation.

When used as a separator, 1·500 kg would be used in preference to 1·5 kg, for instance, and £3·50 rather than £3·5.

Whilst experimenting with the calculator, the children will have seen numbers on the display with many digits after the decimal point. They may well have explored the 'pattern' of some of these decimal numbers (for example, dividing by three can produce a lot of 3s or 6s after the decimal point). This module is mainly concerned with developing the notational aspect of decimal numbers.

Digit cards   The children use digit cards with a decimal point card.

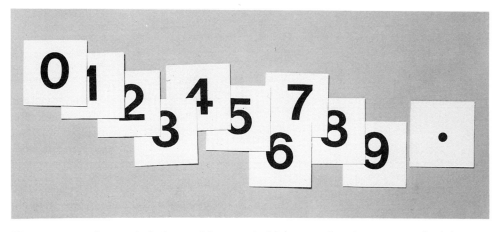

They arrange the cards in front of them or hold them up in a fan as part of a 'show me' activity:
'Show me a number between 2 and 3.'
'Show me seven-tenths.'
'Show me two and a half.'

'Show me 1·6. Make it 2 more.'
'Show me 1·6. Make it 0·2 more.'
'Divide 3 by 10. Show me the answer.'
'Multiply 0·7 by 10. Show me the answer.'

Divide it   The children use a calculator.

'The answer is 0·5.
Which number could have been divided by which number to give this answer?
What do you notice about the two numbers?'
(Answer: one is double the other.)

'The answer is 0·2.
Which number could have been divided by which number to give this answer?
What do you notice about the two numbers?'
(Answer: the dividing number is 5 or a multiple of 5.)

Number lines   What does each dot stand for?

0 1

0 . . . 1 2

0 . 1 . 2 . 3 . 4 . 5

Place the number   Use number lines which do not have intermediate points marked.
The children have to estimate the position of the decimal numbers.

0   1
_____

Where does 0·5 go?
Where does 0·2 go?
Where does 0·7 go?

0   1   2
_____

Where does 1·3 go?
Where does 0·6 go?
Where does 1·9 go?

Grids   Use 'small' squared paper (for example, 2 mm squared).

The children colour the paper to represent decimal numbers.

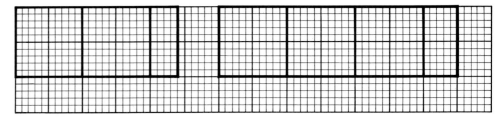

'Show 2·4.'   'Show 3·5.'

Nearest whole This can be a mental activity or decimal number lines can be used:

0 . . . . 1 . . . . 2 3

Give a decimal number and ask the children to say which whole number it is nearest. If it is exactly half way, they should say 'half way'.

'Which whole number is 2·4 nearest?'
'Which whole number is 0·7 nearest?'
'Which whole number is 4·5 nearest?'

Lines The children draw lines which are of a specified length, say 3·6 cm, 6·9 cm and 8·5 cm.

Money

Whilst the children are working on the money modules in *Peak Two* (parts 1 and 2) they will have experience of activities which:

● encourage appropriate calculation methods in money problems
● use an investigatory approach.

Many of the suggested activities assume that the children have access to real (or play) coins.

Check that sensible number processes are being applied when children are solving word problems, for example, that multiplication is used rather than repeated addition.

Much of the work connected with money is concerned with oral and mental numerical skills. The children should have as many opportunities as possible to practise and develop these.

Coin challenges Encourage the children to look for as many different solutions as possible. They should not stop when one solution has been found.

There are three coins in a purse.
They are all worth the same.
What amounts could there be?

There are three coins in a tin.
They are all different.
What amounts could there be?

How many ways can £1 be made with:
5 coins
6 coins?

What is the smallest number of coins needed to make £1 when:
all the coins are different?
there is an equal number of silver and bronze coins?

What amounts up to £1 cannot be made with:

You have one of each coin up to 50p.
What amounts of money can you make?

You have one silver and two bronze coins.
What amounts can you make?

In a purse there are six coins.
All the coins are silver.
What is the most they can be worth?
What is the least they can be worth?

Six coins are worth £2·10.
They are all silver coins.
What could they be?

Which coins?
£2·50   5 coins
£3·20   6 coins
£0·65   7 coins

Guess the coins

An activity for two children.

One child tells the other how many coins he or she has in his or her hand. The second child has to work out their value, asking as few questions as possible. The child with the coins can only answer 'Yes' or 'No'.

Possible questions
Are any of them silver? (Yes)
Are they all silver? (Yes)
Are they all different? (No)
Are two the same? (Yes)
Are there any round coins? (No)
Do they total over £1? (Yes)
The total must be £1·20. (2 × 50p, 1 × 20p)

Measures

Length

Whilst the children are working on the length modules in *Peak Two* (parts 1 and 2) they will have experience of activities in which they:

- measure with centimetres and metres
- measure to the nearest metre/centimetre
- draw lines of stated length accurately
- are encouraged to estimate
- use a wide range of measuring instruments
- measure perimeters and circumferences
- use metre notation (for example, 4·25 m)
- use equivalences between centimetres and metres.

Through discussion, try to develop the children's ability to discriminate between situations where precision is necessary and those where a more approximate measurement is appropriate. For example, is it necessary to include centimetres when measuring the length of the playground or would you measure to the nearest metre?

Peak Plus The following pages from *Peak Plus 2* may be appropriate for children investigating length activities.

Mystery tours   page 8
Postcards   page 30
Link-up   page 36

Peak Posters The Peak Posters 'Curves' and 'Distortion' can be used as starting points for some length activities.

Shape perimeter The children use a collection of plane shapes.

Which shape has the greatest perimeter?

Paper strips The children use long thin strips of paper.
They put the strip round various items and cut off a length equal to the perimeter.
A graph can be created using these strips.

Perimeters

Items measured

| Jar |
| Box |
| Beaker |

Distance round

String perimeters The child cuts four identical lengths of string or wool.
He or she sticks these lengths on to paper to make different shapes.
Discussion should emphasise that different shapes can have the same perimeter.
Areas could be compared if you wish.

Squares perimeters

Which combination of six squares gives the greatest perimeter?
Which gives the smallest perimeter?
The children should try with other numbers of squares.
Is there a rule?

The perimeters can be compared without measuring in cm. For example:
the 'steps' perimeter = 12 units
the 2 × 3 rectangle perimeter = 10 units
the 1 × 6 rectangle perimeter = 14 units

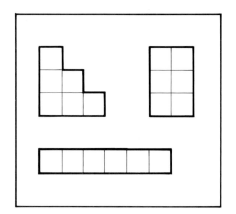

Triangles perimeters

Similar work to that in the previous activity can be done on isometric paper. Which combination of six triangles gives the greatest perimeter?

Hexagon paper can also be used.

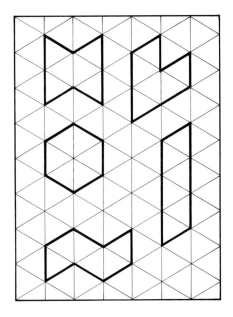

Paper folding

The children measure the distance round a piece of paper.
They fold the paper in half.
'How far is it round the paper now?'
'Is it half the previous distance?'
The children halve the paper a different way (for example, diagonally).
'How far is it round the paper now?'
'Is it the same as before?'
'Is it half the distance this time?'

The children repeat the activity, folding the piece of paper into quarters.

49

Cube measuring   What is the shortest distance round a cube?
What is the longest distance using 4 straight lines only?

Geoboards   The children make squares with perimeters of different sizes on a 9-pin board.
'How many different perimeters can be made?'

They could try the same on a 16-pin board and on boards of other sizes.

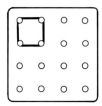 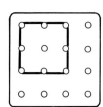 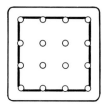

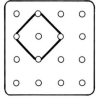 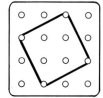 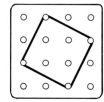

The children make quadrilaterals with different perimeters on a 16-pin board.
'Which quadrilateral has the largest perimeter? Do not forget the concave quadrilaterals.'

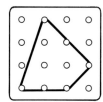

The children find the longest route which visits every pin on a 9-pin geoboard once.
There must be no crossings.
They could use string and measure the distance.

Let them do the same to find the shortest route.

They could do the same activity using a 16-pin board.

About yourself 'Is your cubit the same measurement as your waist?'
'Are you taller than your fathom?'
'Is your head circumference longer than from your knee to your heel?'
'Is your trunk as long as your leg?'

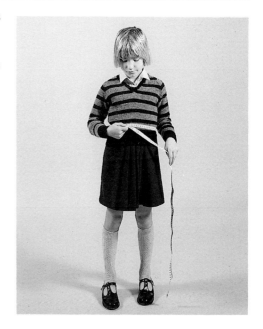

Jumps 'Make one jump from a mark on the floor and measure it.'
'Calculate how far 5 jumps will take you.'
'Make the jumps and measure.'
Discuss with the child the reason for the difference in the two results.

Similar activities can be done involving hopping, striding and so on.
'Make 2 marks on the playground a distance apart. (Suggest 15 m.)
Make one jump from the first mark and then estimate how many more jumps will be needed to reach the other mark.'
Repeat this activity for hops and strides.

Bolts Make a collection of bolts and nuts
which fit them.
The child measures a bolt and
estimates how many complete turns of
the nut will take it to the top. (Colour one
side of the nut for ease of counting.)
Does the length of the bolt determine
how many turns of the nut are needed to
reach the top?

Curve stitching Simple curve stitching involves accurate measurement along the axes.

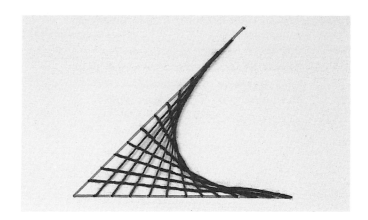

Weight

Whilst the children are working on the weight modules in *Peak Two* (parts 1 and 2) they will have experience of activities in which they:

● weigh and balance with grams and kilograms
● use scales
● use the equivalence between kilograms and grams
● use kilogram notation (for example, 2·750 kg)
● are encouraged to estimate
● consider conservation of weight
● compare weight with volume.

Although there is a scientific difference between weight and mass, and strictly speaking 'mass' is the correct term to use in many of these activities, it has been decided to keep to the more commonly used and understood term 'weight' throughout the pupil and teacher texts.

There is a difference between weighing and balancing activities. In weighing, the children place the object to be weighed on the scales and then add the weights. In balancing they will place the weight(s) on the scales and then add the item until it balances the weight(s) (as in baking activities). In real life, balancing is more often undertaken than weighing.

When weighing an object, using a balance and weights, the technique of adding weights to the balance needs to be discussed. Many children will add a succession of small weights instead of starting with the largest appropriate weight.

When weighing objects on compression scales, the value of the divisions between the marked weights should be discussed.

Peak Plus The following page from *Peak Plus 2* may be appropriate for children investigating early ideas of weighing and balancing.

Weigh it   page 16

Calculate the weight Weigh 5 conkers.
Calculate the weight of 20 conkers.
Weigh 20 conkers.
Are your two results the same?
(Discuss the discrepancy with the child.)

Weigh 10 marbles.
Calculate the weight of one marble.
Weigh one marble.
Were you correct?

How many?

Weigh 50 g of dog biscuits.
How many biscuits are there?
Can you calculate how many you would
get in 500 g?

How many bolts are there in 50 g?
How many screws are there in 50 g?
How many will there be in 1 kg?

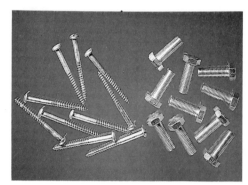

Display

Make a display of items where the weights shown on the labels use different
notations

The items can be used for ordering by size and by weight.

Postage The cost of posting parcels of different weights could be shown on a card.
The children decide how much it would cost to send each parcel.

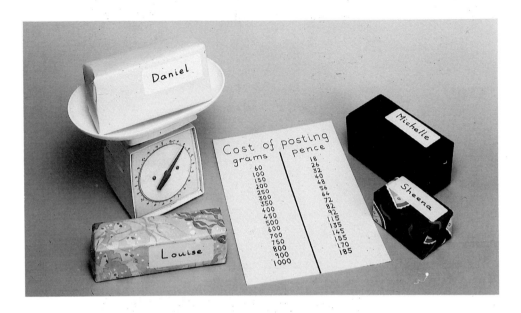

Capacity

Whilst the children are working on the capacity modules in *Peak Two* (parts 1 and 2) they will have experience of activities in which they:

- find capacity in litres and millilitres
- use the equivalence between litres and millilitres
- use litre notation (for example, 1·250 l)
- are encouraged to estimate
- consider conservation of capacity.

When the children are using graduated jugs or cylinders they will need to understand the value of the intermediate divisions between the marked capacities.

Graduated bottles The children can make their own graduated measure by pouring known amounts of water into a plastic bottle and marking the sides. Parallel-sided bottles are the most suitable.

The children can then use the measuring cylinder for practical activities:
Collect five containers.
Estimate the capacity of each one.
Use the measuring cylinder to check your estimates.

Looks different   Pour the same quantity of water into plastic bottles of different shapes.
Mark the water level in each.
Cut the tops off at this mark to create containers of the same capacity. The children
can use these containers in comparison activities.

Check point   Make a collection of commercial
containers where the capacity is shown
on the label.

The stated capacity can be checked.
Usually the containers hold more than is
stated on the label.
Discuss why some bottles may not be
filled to the top. Perhaps it makes them
look better bargains if the container is
larger.

On some labels centilitres (cl) are used.
The relationship of centilitres to
millilitres and litres can be discussed
and explored.

Some labels show imperial units as well
as metric. These can be discussed and
explored.

Capacity weights   This practical work links capacity and
weight.

'Find the weight of 2 flat tablespoonsful
of sand.'
'Find the weight of 2 flat tablespoonsful
of rice.'

Similar activities can be based on
amounts measured in a measuring
cylinder or jug.
'What does 100 ml of sand weigh?'
'Calculate the weight of 200 ml of sand.'
'Check your answer by weighing 200 ml
of sand.'

Dosage How many doses of medicine are in the
bottle?
(Doses could vary if you wish.)
How long will it last?

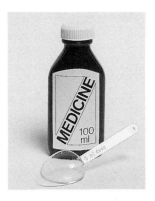

Area

Whilst the children are working on the area modules in *Peak Two* (parts 1 and 2)
they will have experience of activities which:

- involve covering surfaces with a variety of shapes
- develop ideas of conservation of area
- allow them to find area by counting squares
- encourage estimation skills
- introduce the notation cm².

Many tessellation activities can be used as an introduction to the concept of
area.

The shapes whose areas are being measured include non-regular shapes,
showing that area is not necessarily 'length times breadth'. When finding the
area of non-regular shapes, the issue of how to deal with 'partial squares' round
the edges will arise naturally. The suggested rule to use in these circumstances
is:
If it is more than half a square call it a whole one.
If it is less than half a square ignore it.
This rule should be discussed with the children.

Although the standard unit of measurement (cm²) is introduced in *Peak Two
part 2*, the general term 'square units' can still be used in many of the activities.
In particular, many geoboard investigations lend themselves to working in
'square units' rather than cm².

When finding the area of classroom objects such as desk or table tops, you may
feel that it is appropriate to use the square decimetre (dm²) as a unit of
measurement. Measuring in cm² and m² only can be restricting.

Peak Plus The following pages from *Peak Plus 2* may be appropriate for children investigating
early ideas of area.

How many? The children should cover a whole range of surfaces with a variety of tessellating shapes to see how many are needed. They should be encouraged to estimate before counting. Discussion will be needed as to how to deal with the 'bits' around the edges of the surface being covered.

How many rectangles cover the book?
How many triangles cover the book?
How many hexagons cover the book?
How many squares cover the book?

Draw round a shoe.
How many rectangles cover the shoe?
How many triangles cover the shoe?
How many squares cover the shoe?
How many hexagons cover the shoe?

Shape areas The children find the areas of various shapes.
They could use squared paper or transparent grids.
The squares on the paper should be a suitable size.

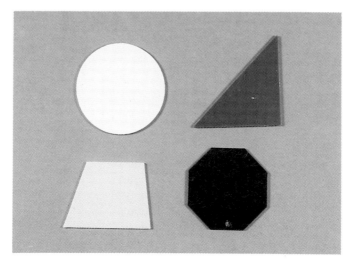

Triangles   The children make a triangle on a 16-pin board.
They make another triangle of the same area.
This can be repeated for other shapes.
The results can be shown on spotty paper.

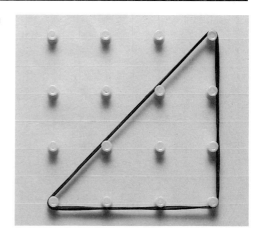

Tangrams   Different shaped tangrams can help to develop the concept of conservation of area.
The children make a whole range of shapes with the tangram.

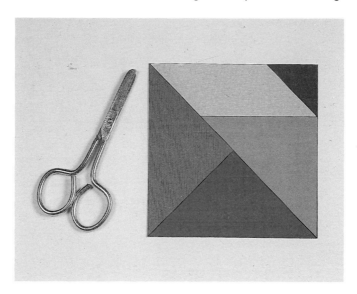

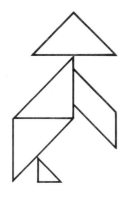 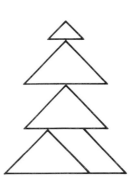 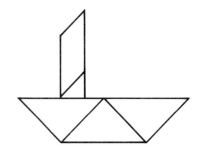

Ominoes   Use four triangles.
Make different shapes with them.

Use four squares.
Make different shapes with them.

Use four rectangles.
Make different shapes with them.

Standard units

The following activities can be based on standard units.

Grids   Allow the child as many opportunities as possible to estimate and count the areas of familar shapes (for example, hand, foot, round shapes). A transparent grid (cm²) is needed for counting.

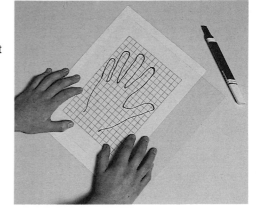

Rectangles On cm squared paper, the children draw as many different rectangles as they can with an area of 24 cm².

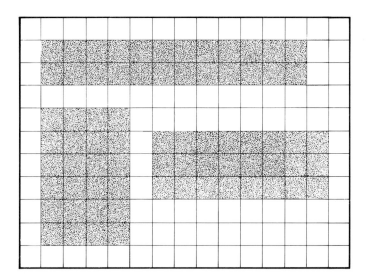

Geostrips The children use geostrips.
They make different shapes and draw round the inside of each.
Then they find the areas.

The children make a square or rectangle, then slope the shape.
Does the area change?
As you slope the shape more, what happens to the area? (It reduces.)
When do you get the largest area?

Constant area The children produce different pictures and shapes, each with an area of 40 cm².
The pictures can be drawn on cm² paper or cut from an 8 cm × 5 cm rectangle.

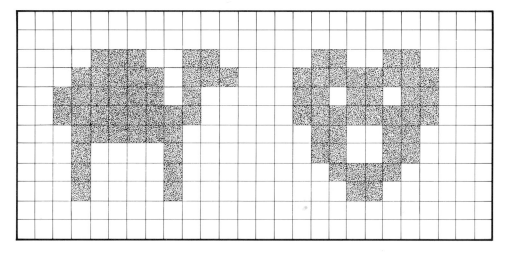

Decimetres The children find the areas of a variety of surfaces around the classroom using a 10 cm × 10 cm square.

Angles

Whilst the children are working on the angles modules in *Peak Two* (parts 1 and 2) they will have experience of activities which develop several aspects of turning and direction:

- turning – right angles, more than a right angle, less than a right angle, fractions of a turn
- personal directions – left, right, front, back
- impersonal directions – compass directions, clockwise, anti-clockwise

The early work on angles concentrates upon an angle as an amount of turn and on recognising right angles.

The children will use a magnetic compass and a set square during the course of the modules.

Peak software   The following computer programs allow the children to explore turns and angles. The first program in each suite of three is a teaching program which should be used with the teacher. The other programs are for the children to use.

'Directions One' programs

Follow the road

Keep on the path

Steer the boat

'Directions Two' programs

Face the right way

Which way to turn?

Get Donna home

Going Home

'Directions Three' programs

The eight compass points

More ways to turn

Line up your ship

Mind the dog

'Angles One' programs

How much of a turn?

Stop the turn

Skittles

Peak Plus   The following pages from *Peak Plus 2* may be appropriate for children investigating early work on angles, turning and direction.

Mystery tours   page 8
Turning shapes   page 11
Shape shadows   page 28
Triangle mix   page 44

Turtle   One child is blindfolded and is the 'turtle'.
One or two skittles are placed on the playground or in the hall.
The 'turtle' has to be directed round the obstacle with instructions such as:
'Take five strides forward.'
'Turn left.'
'Take three strides forward.'

Routes   Let the children plan routes around the school using a trundle wheel and the language of direction.

1 Begin at the classroom door
2 Turn right
3 Walk 10 metres
4 Turn left
5 Walk 5 metres

Where are you?

1 Begin at the staffroom
2 Turn North
3 Walk 3 metres
4 Turn East
5 Walk 8 metres
6 Turn South
Where are you?

Compasses   The children use a magnetic compass.

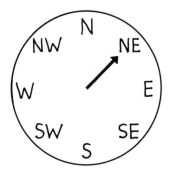

'Face north. What is on your left? right?
behind? in front?'
'Face east. What is on your left? right?
behind? in front?'
This can be repeated for other compass points.
Through discussion the children should come to
realise the difference between 'personal direction'
(left/right) and compass directions.

Discussion on the eight points of the compass can
lead to activities with half right angles.

Right angles   On a 9-pin geoboard, the children make
different right-angled triangles.
How many can they make?

Can they make a four-sided shape
which has:
1 only one right angle in it
2 two right angles in it
3 three right angles in it
4 four right angles in it?

The children should repeat the activity
on a 16-pin geoboard.

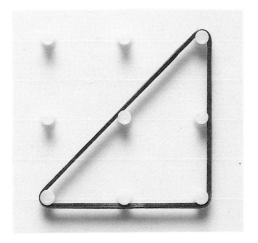

Geostrips   Find geostrips of different lengths.
Fasten them together to make a shape.
Can you twist your shape to create a
right angle?
Rearrange the strips and repeat.

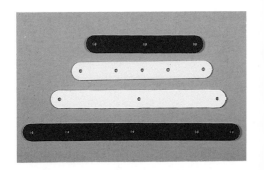

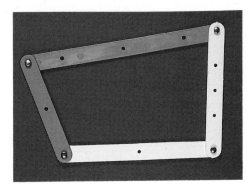

Make a square with geostrips.
Twist the square.
How many angles are there that are
greater than a right angle?
How many are less than a right angle?
Alter the shape several times and
re-test.

The children could try similar activities
with a rectangle.

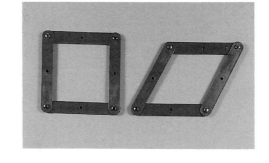

Make a square with geostrips.
Use two more strips to create four more
right angles inside the square.

(Any solution, including the diagonals or
the one opposite, is acceptable.)

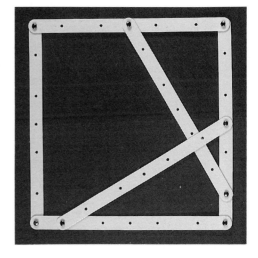

Time

Whilst the children are working on the time modules in *Peak Two* (parts 1 and 2)
they will have experience of activities which develop five aspects of time:

- the concept of time – timing activities, working within a fixed unit of time (for
  example, a minute), a short time ago, a long time ago, quickly, slowly

- functional time – bed time, break time, daytime, night time, evening, morning,
  late, early

- calendar – months, days, seasons, festivals, birthdays, centuries, dates,
  events

- telling the time – oral activities, quarter to, half past, twenty-five to,
  six forty-five, analogue clocks, digital clocks

- recording time – writing times, reading written times, timetables, am, pm,
  calculating intervals of time.

The children should develop the skill of saying what the time is in two ways:
informal, for example, 'It's five to three.'
as written, for example, 'It's two fifty-five.'
In the pupil text the children are not expected to record time in the 'informal'
style.

Peak Explorer Two (parts 1 and 2) These books offer further pupil material involving the processes, skills and language associated with time.

Class Topic Time is suitable as a class topic. Suggested activities for such a theme are given in the *First Resource Book*, page 87.

Pendulum A pendulum can be made by tying a weight to the end of a length of string. The string is fastened by a bulldog clip to a suitable point. The bulldog clip allows the string to be lengthened or shortened easily.

The pendulum can be used to give a fixed period of time against which simple events can be compared. The children can experiment with lengthening and shortening the string. Can a minute timer be made?

Standard timers These devices are based on standard units of time (minutes and seconds). They can be used to compare how long certain activities take to complete.

Special days The following list is a guide to special days and festivals to which you may wish to refer during the course of the school year. Some of the festivals listed fall on specific dates and do not vary. Others fall between given dates and vary from year to year. In some cases (largely Muslim festivals) the festival is held progressively earlier each year.

An up to date list of religious festivals can be obtained from the Shap Working Party, c/o Alan Brown, 23 Kensington Square, London W8 5HN. The list is published by the Commission for Racial Equality, Elliot House, 10–12 Allington Street, London, SW1E 5EH.

January
1   New Year
6   Twelfth Night (Christian)
25 Burns' Night

January/February
Chinese New Year

February
2   Candlemas (Christian)
15 Sarasvati Puja (Hindu)
Shiva Rati (Hindu)

February/March
Shrove Tuesday
Mardi Gras
Lent
Mothering Sunday
Lantern Festival (Chinese)
Holi (Hindu)

March
1   St David's Day
17 St Patrick's Day
21 Spring Equinox

March/April
Commonwealth Day
Good Friday
Easter Sunday
Ramanavmi (Birthday of Lord Rama) (Hindu)

April
1   All Fool's Day
12 Cosmonaut's Day (USSR)
23 St George's Day
Pesakh (Passover) (Jewish)
Start of Ramadan (Muslim)

May
1   May Day
5   Europe Day
8   Red Cross Day
29 Oakapple Day
Eid-ul-fitr (Muslim)
Spring Bank Holiday

May/June
Whitsuntide
Martyrdom of Guru Arjan Dev (Sikh)
Dragon Boat Festival (Chinese)
Father's Day

June
21 Summer Solstice (longest day)
24 Midsummer day

July
4   Independence Day (USA)
15 St Swithin's Day
Eid-ul-adha (Muslim)

August
Al Hijra (Muslim)
Hungry Ghosts Festival (Chinese)

August/September
Janmashtami (Birth of Lord Krishna) (Hindu)

September
15 Battle of Britain Day
29 Michaelmas
Rosh Hashana (New Year) (Jewish)

September/October
Harvest Festival
Durga Puja (Hindu)

October
21 Trafalgar Day
24 United Nations Day
31 Hallow-e'en
Dashara (Hindu)
Yom Kippur (Day of Atonement) (Jewish)

October/November
Divali (Dipavalli or Kali Puja) Indian New year (Hindu and Sikh)
Remembrance Sunday (second Sunday in November)

November		December	

November
5   Bonfire Night
30 St Andrew's Day
Birthday of Guru Nanak (Sikh)

November/December
Thanksgiving Day (USA) (fourth
Thursday in November)
Advent

December
24 Christmas Eve
25 Christmas Day
26 Boxing Day
31 New Year's Eve
    Hogmanay
Hanukah (Jewish)

December/January
Birthday of Guru Gobind Singh (Sikh)

Resources

Brighouse, A., Godber, D. and Patilla, P., *New Peak Stationery Copymasters*,
Thomas Nelson and Sons Ltd, 1990.

Shape and space

Whilst the children are working on the Shape and space modules in *Peak Two* (parts 1 and 2) they will have experience of activities which develop several aspects of Shape and space:

- sorting and classifying
- construction and destruction
- tessellation
- symmetry
- patterns
- shape properties

The children will be working with two dimensional and three dimensional natural and man-made shapes. They will have experience of irregular shapes as well as regular and semi-regular ones.

It is assumed that they will use the glossary at the back of the Pupil's Book for help with the names of shapes and other terms.

The children will be involved in constructions but also in destructions in which shapes are carefully undone to see how they are made.

'Pattern' covers a very wide area of investigation. Included in these modules is the notion of repeating shapes to make a pattern.

It is hoped that the classification of shapes will become a little more sophisticated as the children progress.

Peak Explorer Two (parts 1 and 2)   These books offer further pupil material involving the processes, skills and language associated with shape.

Peak Plus   The following pages from *Peak Plus 2* may be appropriate for children investigating Shape and space.

Peak Posters   The following Peak Posters provide interesting starting points for Shape and space investigations:

Circle patterns	Nets
Curves	Paper threading
Distortion	Star holes
Matchsticks	

Class Topics   There are ideas for Shape and space activities in the class topics 'Faces' and 'Pattern' on pages 78 and 84.

Blots   The children put drops of ink or paint on a sheet of paper.
They fold the paper in half and smooth it out.
They open the paper to reveal a symmetrical shape.

Drawing   The child finishes the drawing.
It must be symmetrical.

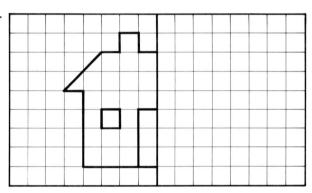

Cutting   The child folds a sheet of paper in half.
He or she cuts a piece out of the folded edge.
The child then draws what he or she thinks the hole will look like when the paper is opened.

Was the child right?

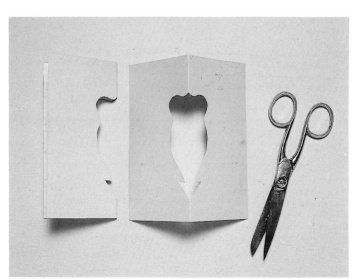

Symmetry in words When a mirror is put in the centre of this word, the word does not change.
The children find other words which do not change. These words have symmetry.

Colouring symmetry The children colour to create a
symmetrical pattern.
This could be extended to make the
pattern have only one line of symmetry
or to make the pattern have two lines of
symmetry.

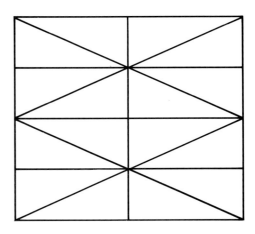

Number symmetry The children colour the multiples of 2 on a 100 square.
How many lines of symmetry can they find?
This can be repeated for other number patterns.

1	2	3	4	5	6	7	8	9	10
11	12	13	14	15	16	17	18	19	20
21	22	23	24	25	26	27	28	29	30
31	32	33	34	35	36	37	38	39	40
41	42	43	44	45	46	47	48	49	50
51	52	53	54	55	56	57	58	59	60
61	62	63	64	65	66	67	68	69	70
71	72	73	74	75	76	77	78	79	80
81	82	83	84	85	86	87	88	89	90
91	92	93	94	95	96	97	98	99	100

Square start   The children start with a square of paper. They colour or cut out one piece to leave only one line of symmetry.

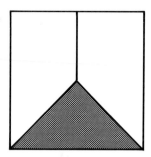

Hexagon cuts   The children cut up regular hexagons.

'Cut up a hexagon to make 6 triangles.'

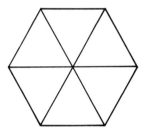

'Cut up a hexagon to make 2 equal triangles and a rectangle.'

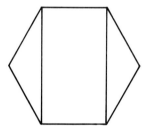

'Cut up a hexagon to make 2 equal triangles and 2 equal rectangles.'

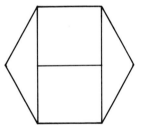

'Cut up a hexagon to make 4 equal triangles and 2 equal rectangles.'

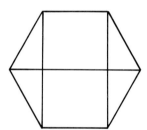

Polygons   'How many different polygons can you make on a 9-pin geoboard? Each polygon must have a different number of sides.'
'How many different polygons can you make on a 16-pin geoboard?'

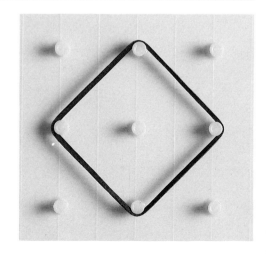

Triangles   The children find as many different triangles as possible on a 9-pin board. (They could record on spotty paper.) Discuss with them what makes the triangles 'different' (for example, shape and size).

Repeat on a 16-pin board.

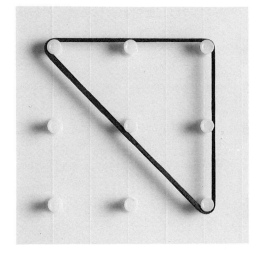

Isosceles triangles   How many different isosceles triangles can be made on a 16-pin board? Solutions may include:

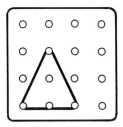 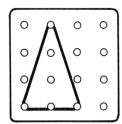 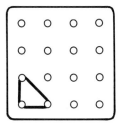

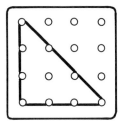 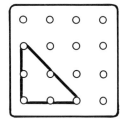 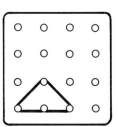

Repeating shapes   'Use spotty paper.
Draw an isosceles triangle.
Repeat the triangle to make a pattern.'

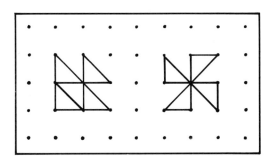

Mirror cards

'Make a "mirror card".
Place a mirror on it.
Which other shapes can be made?'

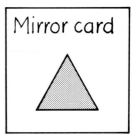

Some possible solutions include:

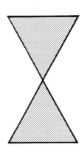  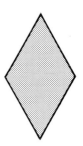

 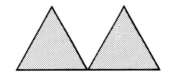 

Diagonals

'Draw a regular hexagon.
Draw some diagonals.
How many different lengths can you find?'

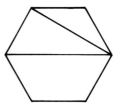

This activity can be repeated with different regular polygons.

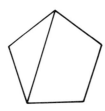 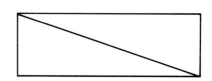

The children could try this with semi-regular polygons.

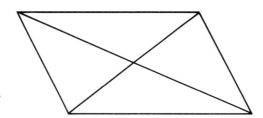

Centre folding   The children find the centres of polygons by folding.

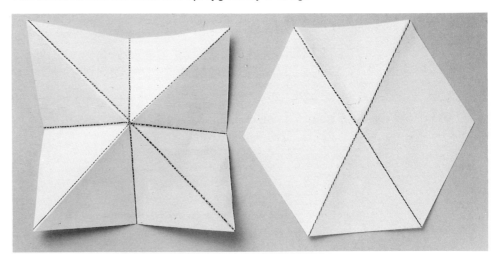

Handling data

Whilst the children are working on the data handling modules in *Peak Two* (parts 1 and 2) they will have experience of activities which develop several aspects of recording and interpreting information. Types of data representation relevant to children at this stage include: pictograms, bar graphs, mappings, matrices, Venn diagrams, Carroll diagrams, tables, charts, networks, sketches, maps and models.

Data handling activities should permeate all the other modules. Ways of representing information should develop out of the children's activities, as well as being taught specifically 'in isolation'.
A discussion of the completed representation and what it shows is of more importance than the actual recording. There is little point in representing data unless the information is going to be used.
The way in which statistical data is collected, recorded, tabulated and presented should develop throughout the school.
The children should be aware of the need for care in labelling axes, choosing a scale, providing a key, and giving the graph or chart a heading.
Occasionally the children should be encouraged to represent the same data in a variety of ways to highlight the fact that there is not always 'one best way'.

Peak Plus   The following pages from *Peak Plus 2* may be appropriate for children investigating the representation of information.

Probabilities

Encourage the children of investigate and discuss ideas of likelihood and fairness, by experimenting with coins, dice, playing cards and dominoes.

Using dice

a) Which is the most likely to turn up – an odd or even number?

b) Is there a fair chance of any number being rolled?

c) Is there more or less than an even chance of rolling a six?

d) Roll two dice. Which total is most likely to occur? What are the possibilities?

Using playing cards

a) Turn over a card. Is there an even chance of it being:
  – an odd number?   – a red card?

b) Use a probability scale to predict the likelihood of it being:
  – a heart   – a picture card
  – a club   – the four of clubs
  – an even card

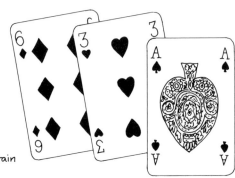

Probability scale

Using coins

Toss 2 coins. Which combinations of Heads and Tails are possible?
Which is most likely to occur?
Compile a frequency table to over 50 throws.

	FREQUENCY	TOTAL
H. H.	IIII	
T. T.	ＨＨＴ II	
H. T.	ＨＨＴ	

Will 100 throws give a more predictable result?

Using dominoes

Children can list possible outcomes of activities such as:

a) What are the possible totals on individual dominoes?

b) Which totals occur most/least often?

c) Choose any two dominoes from a pack placed face down. What is the likelihood of their total being:
  – one?   – less than thirty-two?
  – thirty-five? – thirteen
  – over five?

Use a probability scale to indicate likelihood.

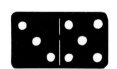

Total 8

Total 7

Bookshelves The diagrams below show information gathered about the books on a bookshelf in a classroom. They indicate some different ways of representing the information. It can be seen that the method of presentation can vary considerably. Each format emphasises a particular aspect of the information.

1 The list gives precise details of the books.
2 The horizontal column graph gives information on the number of pages in the books available.
3 The vertical column graph shows which publishers are most popular when ordering books for the class.
4 The matrix shows the sizes and heights of books placed in the bookcase.

List of books on class bookshelf

Title	Publisher	Type
All about me	Nelson	Non fiction
Animal world	Hamlyn	Non fiction
Book of Giant Stories	Jonathan Cape	Fiction
Coal in Britain	Cassell	Non fiction
Dragon's Birthday	Ginn	Fiction
Edwardian Costumes	Jonathan Cape	Non fiction
Egg in the Hole	Hamlyn	Fiction
Food for thought	Nelson	Non fiction
Good Health	Nelson	Non fiction
Inside a Victorian House	Jonathan Cape	Non fiction
Little Red Fox	Oliver and Boyd	Fiction
Living Countryside	Cassell	Non fiction
Lucky Feather	Ginn	Fiction
Magic Mill	Ginn	Fiction
Meg's Castle	Oliver and Boyd	Fiction
Mouse Deer's Market	Ginn	Fiction
Mr. Grumpy's motor car	Oliver and Boyd	Fiction
Muhammad	Cassell	Non fiction
Musical Instruments	Oliver and Boyd	Non fiction
Peak 3	Nelson	Non fiction
Pond Life	Oliver and Boyd	Non fiction
Porcellus the Flying Pig	Jonathan Cape	Fiction
Sebastian	Hamlyn	Fiction
Space	Hamlyn	Non fiction
The Spider and the Shower	Ginn	Fiction
Tiny Tales	Cassell	Fiction
Tom Thumb	Hamlyn	Fiction
Tortoise's Dream	Ginn	Fiction
Water	Cassell	Non fiction

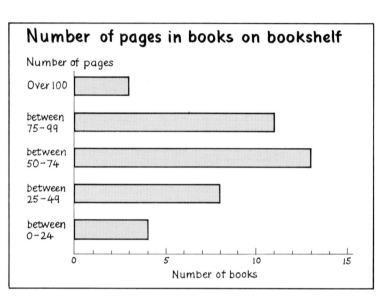

Number of pages in books on bookshelf

Number of books and publishers on bookshelf

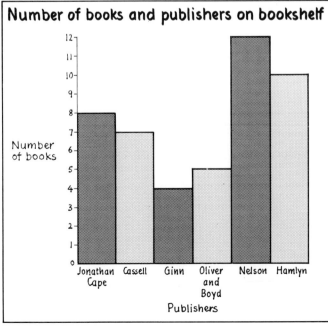

Sizes and heights of books on bookshelf

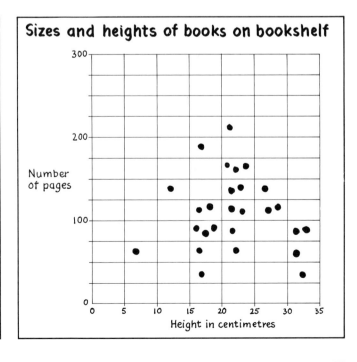

Class topics

The ideas suggested on the following pages give an opportunity to develop a mathematical theme with a whole class or group, even though the ability range within the class or group is fairly wide. The activities have been selected to develop positive attitudes in children towards mathematics by offering them the following learning experiences:

- involvement in activities which are short in duration as well as those which can be developed into extended pieces of work
- an opportunity to communicate about their work
- activities through which they can acquire knowledge skills and understanding and develop the ability to solve problems
- involvement in tasks which are of an open-ended type, as well as those which have a single solution
- an opportunity to bring together different areas of mathematics
- an opportunity to use a range of mathematical tools
- an opportunity to work independently, in groups, and as a class.

The suggested topics are:
Faces   Patterns   Fractions

Faces

Faces and shapes

The children use Clixi or Polydron apparatus.
They are asked to make shapes with special face attributes:

'Make shapes which have two triangle faces. Other shapes can be used as well.'

'Make shapes which have only triangle and pentagon faces.'

'Make shapes with triangle faces only.'

How many faces? The children use Clixi or Polydron apparatus.
They make shapes which have four faces, five faces, six faces, and so on.

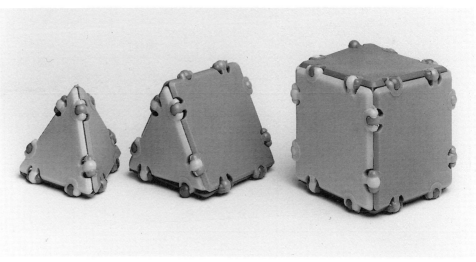

Polyhedra The children could use their reference skills to collect the names of polyhedra. They could also make some of them:

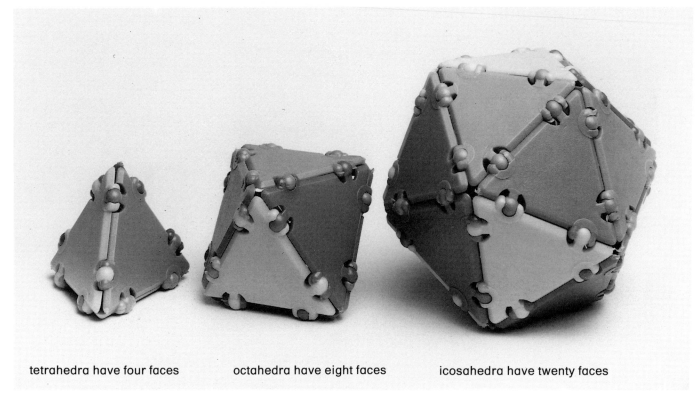

tetrahedra have four faces   octahedra have eight faces   icosahedra have twenty faces

and so on.

Symmetrical faces Symmetrical faces can be made from two sheets of card of different colours.

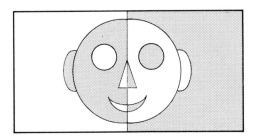

Curve stitching Faces can be made from curve stitching.

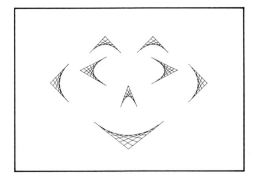

Distortions   The children could make distorted faces on various grids.

Painted face problem   A 3 × 3 × 3 cube is painted red.
It is then cut up into 27 smaller cubes.
How many cubes have paint:
on one face?
on two faces?
on no faces?

The children could try different sized
starting cubes.
They could try cuboids.

Rubik's cube   The children could experiment to get
different colour combinations on each
face.

Clockfaces   Each child is given or makes a card clockface.
The children show various times on their clockfaces according to the questions
asked:
show a quarter past three
show fifteen minutes later
show an hour before.

Playing cards The children use a complete set of the picture cards.

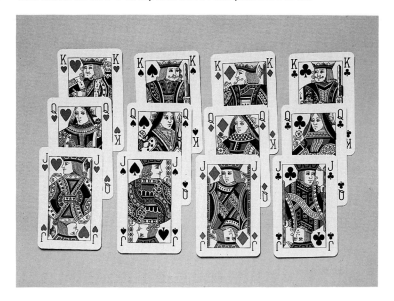

They make up quiz questions based on the faces:
Which face has two rows of curls?
Which face has a leaf?
Which faces look to the left?
Which face holds a sword vertically?

Challenge the children to make up a set of questions which will identify each card.

Faces on dice Dice faces can be used to provide simple problems.
Most of the solutions depend upon the children 'discovering' that the opposite faces of a dice total seven.

Roll four dice.
How many spots are touching the table?

Put four dice in a line.
How many spots are hidden?

Put a dice between two hinged mirrors.
What is the largest number of dots you can see?

Faces on dominoes   Problems and investigations based on the faces of dominoes can be found in the
peak mathematics scheme as follows:

Domino Squares   Peak Poster

Domino squares   *Peak Plus 3*, page 21
Spotty totals   *Peak Plus 4*, page 7

Peak Plus   There are several ideas in the *Peak Plus* books which might be included in a Faces
theme:

Time rocker   *Peak Plus 1*, page 38
Turning shapes   *Peak Plus 2*, page 11
Shadow shapes   *Peak Plus 2*, page 12
Shape shadows   *Peak Plus 2*, page 28
Silhouettes   *Peak Plus 2*, page 29
Puzzle cube   *Peak Plus 3*, page 36
Make a shape   *Peak Plus 4*, page 5

References and resources

Golick, M., *Learning Through Card Games*, Wolfe
Making Shapes booklets from Tarquin Publications

From E J Arnold (Stationery and Equipment)
Clixi
Polydron
Nets of shapes

From Hestair Hope
Polydron

Pattern

This collection of ideas on the theme of Pattern only looks at repeating patterns.

Wrapping paper

Make a display of attractive wrapping papers which have repeating patterns. The children could then make their own wrapping paper using various printing techniques.

The repeat pattern can be based on:

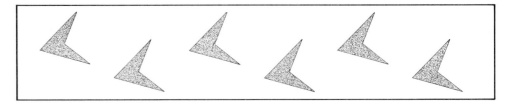

translations (moving the basic shape without turning or reflecting it)

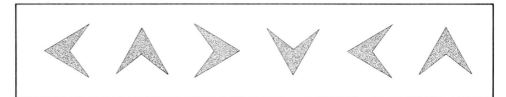

rotations

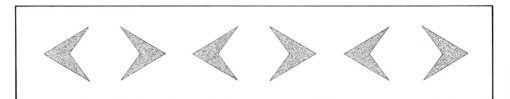

reflections

Concertina figures

Islamic designs

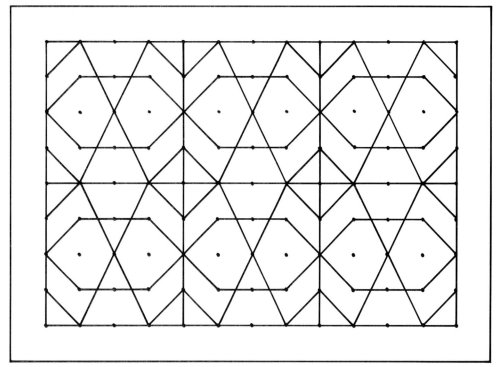

Tessellations

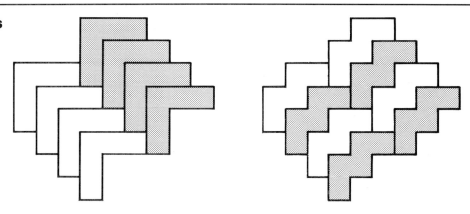

Friezes

Friezes can be made by sliding, rotating or reflecting a simple basic design.

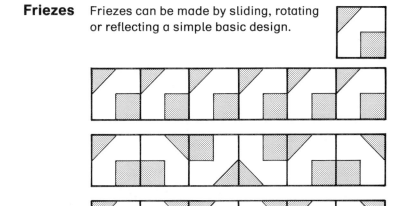

Floors and walls   Look at different brick bondings and tile patterns.

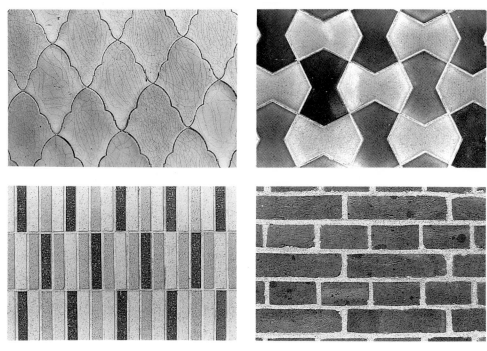

The children could make rubbings.
They could create their own patterns for walls and floors using a variety of materials such as Lego and plastic rectangles and triangles.

Embroidery   Repeating patterns can be built up using embroidery stitches.

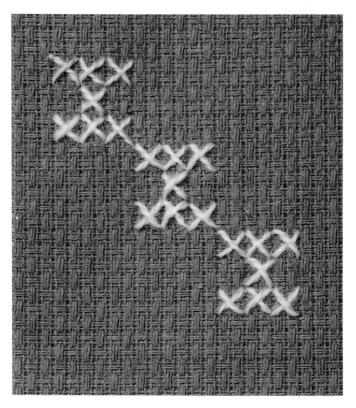

Patchwork   Patchwork is made from repeated patterns. The patchwork can be made from coloured paper or from fabric.

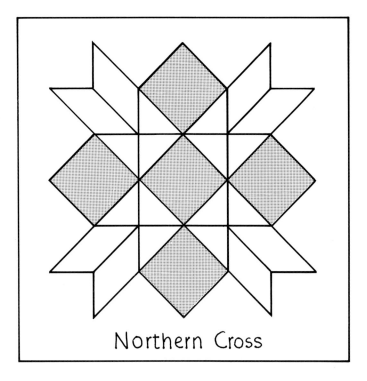

Northern Cross

A large paper patchwork pattern makes an effective background for displaying the children's work on pattern.

Paper threading   The Peak Poster 'Paper Threading' gives ideas for this activity.

Elevens   The 11 × table produces a simple repeat pattern to 11 × 9:

11 22 33 44 55 66 77 88 99

Calculator   The children can experiment to find operations which result in a single digit repeat on the display.

Table repeats   For this the children have to find the digital roots of numbers:

number	add the digits	digital root
24	2 + 4	6
35	3 + 5	8
98	9 + 8 = 17; 1 + 7	8
142	1 + 4 + 2	7

The children can then find which answers to the table facts produce a repeating pattern of digital roots. The simplest patterns are from the $9\times$, $3\times$ and $6\times$ tables.

$9\times$	digital root	$3\times$	digital root	$6\times$	digital root
9	9	3	3	6	6
18	9	6	6	12	3
27	9	9	9	18	9
36	9	12	3	24	6
45	9	15	6	30	3
54	9	18	9	36	9
63	9	21	3	42	6
72	9	24	6	48	3
81	9	27	9	54	9
90	9	30	3	60	6
99	9	33	6	66	3
108	9	36	9	72	9
117	9	39	3	78	6
126	9	42	6	84	3
135	9	45	9	90	9

Peak Plus   There are several ideas in the *Peak Plus* books which might be included in a Pattern theme:

Tissue shapes	*Peak Plus 1* page 7
Exploring circles	*Peak Plus 1* pages 16 and 17
Mind that gap	*Peak Plus 2* pages 4 and 5
Cut it out	*Peak Plus 2* page 17
Joined pairs	*Peak Plus 2* pages 20 and 21
Pattern making	*Peak Plus 2* page 24
Four-in-one	*Peak Plus 4* page 13
Weaving strips	*Peak Plus 4* page 21
Twist and turn	*Peak Plus 4* pages 40 and 41

Peak Posters   Peak Posters which might be used in a Patterns theme are:

Circle patterns
Paper threading
Star holes

References and resources

Ball, J., *Think Box*, Puffin Books, 1982

Bezuszka, S., Kenny, M. and Silvey, L., *Designs from Mathematical Patterns*, Creative Publications (Jonathan Press), 1978

Bourgoin, J., *Arabic Geometrical Pattern and Design*, Dover Publications, 1973

Brandreth, G., *Numberplay*, Severn House, 1985

Dye, D. S., *The New Book of Chinese Lattice Designs*, Dover Publications, 1981

Haig, J. and Webber, B., 'Thought Patterns', *Child Education*, February 1988

Horemis, S., *Optical and Geometric Patterns and Designs*, Dover Publications, 1970

Horemis, S., *Geometrical Design Colouring Book,* Dover Publications, 1973

Oliver, J., *Polysymetrics*, Tarquin Publications

Ouchi, H., *Japanese Optical and Geometric Art*, Dover Publications, 1977

Ranucci, E. R. and Teeters, J. L., *Creating Escher-Type Drawings*, Creative Publications (Jonathan Press), 1977

Roper, A. and Harvey, L., *The Pattern Factory*, Creative Publications (Jonathan Press), 1980

Silvey, L. and Pasternack, M., *Pattern Blocks Colouring Book*, Creative Publications (Jonathan Press), 1974

'Patterns', *Junior Education*, November 1987

'Patterns', Topic Pack from *Junior Education*, August 1986

Software

'Mosaic', Hilditch Software

'Take Half', Micro Smile

'Tessellations', Cambridge University Press

Fractions

These activities explore fractions in different ways. Each may be tackled at several different skill and concept levels.

Several aspects of fractions are considered:
as part of a shape
as part of a quantity
division aspect
position on a number line.

A half

Colour half 'Draw round a shape on plain paper.
Colour half its area.
How many ways can you find?'

'Try a parallelogram.'
'Try any quadrilateral.'

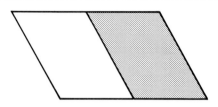

Squared paper 'Draw a 5 × 5 square on cm squared paper.
Find different ways of showing a half.'

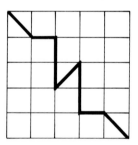

Halves with the same shape and area.

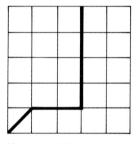

Halves with equal areas but not the same shape.

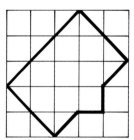

A shape which halves the area.

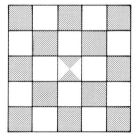

A pattern which halves the area.

The Peak Poster 'Halving' can be used as a starting point.

Geoboard The children make shapes on a 9-pin geoboard.
Each shape must cover half the board.

Try different sized geoboards.

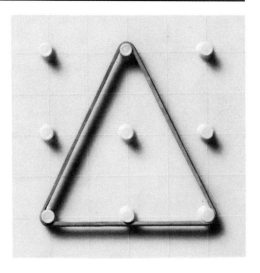

Isometric/dotty paper The children draw shapes on isometric or dotty paper to find different ways of showing a half.

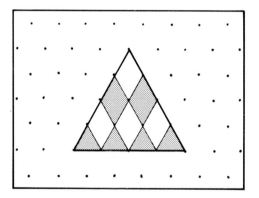

Halves and wholes 'Here is half of a shape.
Draw what the whole shape could look like.'

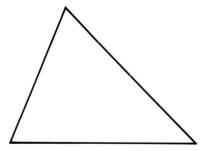

Cuisenaire rods 'Choose any Cuisenaire rod.
Find a rod which is half of it.
Which rods do not have halves?'

Pegboard 'Make a pattern with 12 pegs.
Copy it on spotty paper.
Take away half of the pegs.
Copy the new pattern.'

Half words 'This word is made of half letters.
It is a horizontal half word.'

'What does the word say?
Find other horizontal half words.'

'Find vertical half words.'

'Can you write a sentence with half words?'

Cubes 'Take a handful of cubes.
Count and record how many.
Remove half of them.
How many are you left with?'

Calculator, odd numbers 'Use a calculator.
Enter any odd number.
Find a half of it.
Do this a few times more.
What do you notice about the answers?'

Calculator, halves 'Use a calculator.
Enter any whole number.
Write down what you think a half of it is.
Check to see if you were correct.'

Apples
'Find a half of an apple.
Can you do it exactly?
How can you check?'

Halving in social situations could lead to a discussion about being fair. A balance could be used to check the accuracy of the halving.

Water
The children have two different-shaped containers.
One is full of water.
Can they halve the quantity?
How can they check?

Number lines
Which number does each arrow point to?

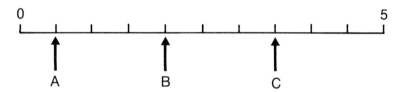

Beyond a half

Cuisenaire rods
'Choose any two Cuisenaire rods.
Write one as a fraction of the other.
Prove you are correct.'

Geoboard
'Use a 9-pin geoboard.
Make different quadrilaterals.
What fraction of the board is each quadrilateral?'

Grids 'Draw a 3 × 4 grid on squared paper.
Divide the grid into equal parts.
You can only draw along the lines.
Which fractions can you show?

Try different grids.'

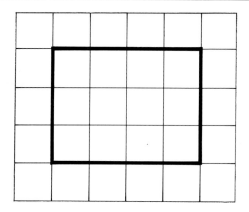

Five-eighths 'Here is a five-eighths pattern.
Make some of your own.'

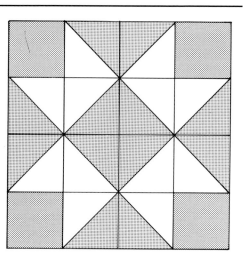

Decimal elevenths 'Use a calculator.
Change one-eleventh into a decimal.
Repeat for the next two members of the eleventh family.
Predict the pattern for the rest of the family.
Check your prediction.'

Calculator 'Use a calculator.
Which fractions produce these decimals:
0·1111111 0·2222222 0·3333333
Will this pattern continue?'

Water 'You have three identical jars.
There are no other containers.
How can you fill each exactly three-quarters full?
How many ways can you find?'

Three-quarters   Colour three-quarters of these:

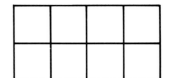

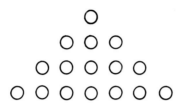
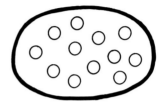

Cuckoos   Find the cuckoos in the nests:

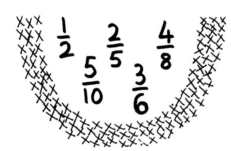
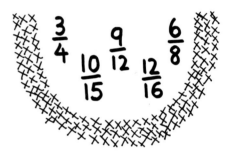

Calculator   'Use a calculator.
Enter whole numbers.
Divide each number by 5 and look at the numbers after the decimal point.
What do you notice?

Try dividing by 3.
What do you notice?

Try dividing by other numbers.'

Number line   Which number does each arrow point to?

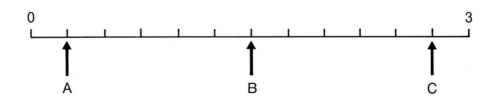

Peak Plus   There are several ideas in the *Peak Plus* books which might be included in a Fractions theme:

Parts of shapes	*Peak Plus 1* pages 34 and 35
Quarter it	*Peak Plus 2* page 13
Halves and quarters	*Peak Plus 2* page 27
Rod pairs	*Peak Plus 2* page 42
Hole in the middle	*Peak Plus 3* page 46
Same but different	*Peak Plus 4* page 8
Fraction patterns	*Peak Plus 4* page 10

Peak Posters   A Peak Poster which might be used in a Fractions theme is 'Halving'.

Resources

Brighouse, A., Godber, D. and Patilla, P., *New Peak Stationery Copymasters*, Thomas Nelson and Sons Ltd, 1990.

Using peak mathematics

The materials within **peak mathematics** closely match the requirements of the National Curriculum.

When starting to use the scheme in school, teachers need as much information as possible about it. In this section we give answers to the questions most commonly asked by teachers about **peak mathematics**.

Starting the scheme

How should peak mathematics be introduced in the school?

Most of the activities in **peak mathematics** are familiar to teachers, and adoption of the scheme does not demand a completely different approach to mathematics. The suggested activities are carefully structured and will help with the development of concepts and language and the learning of skills and processes, as well as the ability to apply these skills and processes to new mathematical situations. The scheme can be introduced across a whole school (see the paragraph below concerning the placing of children on the scheme) or, alternatively, can be introduced in the lower part of the school and allowed to 'grow' through the school.

Is a lot of expensive apparatus needed?

No. The majority of the apparatus suggested is found in most classrooms. A full list of the apparatus needed is given on page 99.

Do I need structured number apparatus?

Structured number apparatus is used in the teaching of place value and for the introduction of number operations. Suitable apparatus to use for this work is Dienes MAB materials (base 10) which are available from E J Arnold (Stationery and Equipment).

In other number work, apparatus such as interlocking cubes (for example, Multilink) and number rods (for example, Cuisenaire, Stern) is useful.

How are the books organised?

There are eight core Pupils' Books. After *Book Zero* which deals mainly with place value, there are two books per year for the first two years, and one book per year for the next two years. An extension book is available for those children who require extra work at the top of the school. However, a child's progress in relation to the National Curriculum should determine which book he or she is using at any given time.

Other pupil materials are available which provide further experience alongside the core books. These include *Peak Plus*, the *Number Skills* books and the *Peak Explorers*.

Using the scheme

Must the pages of each book be done consecutively?

Not necessarily. The books are designed to allow flexibility of organisation. (See pages 8 to 13.)

Does one book have to be finished before the next one is started?

It is best if a child completes one book (and its Assessment Test) before going on to the next, as each book assumes that the teaching points in the previous book have been dealt with successfully.

Is there enough experience in the books for all children?

The amount of experience needed by different children varies considerably. However, children of all abilities benefit from having as wide a range of activities as possible. The *Number Skills* books, *Peak Plus* and *Peak Explorers*, together with the additional ideas in this Resource Book provide just such a wide range.

How should the children record their work?

There is no right or wrong way to record; the scheme allows you to choose the method of recording in the light of the school's policy. However, it is important that recording skills are developed as the children progress and that they meet as many different forms of recording as possible. Eventually the children should be able to choose the most appropriate form of recording for each activity.

How do I place children on the scheme?

The Assessment Tests can be used to determine where to place a child on the scheme. Start with the earliest ones, to establish the ground which the child has already covered. If in any Assessment Test the child only gets a question or two wrong, go over the work involved and then proceed to the next Assessment Test. If the child gets a substantial amount of an Assessment Test wrong, this indicates that he or she needs to be placed on the scheme at the level of the previous Assessment Test.

Can existing materials be used alongside peak mathematics?

Yes, existing material can be incorporated into the scheme. In order to do this, analyse the skill/language of the existing materials, and link them up with the appropriate **peak** Pupils' Books. They can then be appropriately labelled and used as supplementary materials.

Assessment and monitoring

How do I monitor each child's progress?

Assessment is a vital part of any mathematics programme and an element of diagnostic testing has been built into this scheme. At the end of each **peak** Pupils' Book (including *Peak Extra*) or at the end of each part of a Pupils' Book, there is an assessment to test the readiness of the child to move on to the next part of the scheme. Once a test, and any further work resulting from the diagnosis of errors made, have been completed, the test can be filed in a child's records. In this way, a complete record of a child's progress through the scheme and the mathematics involved can be built up. (See also 'Testing' on page 12.)

How do I record each child's progress?

The Progress Records are a summary of the concepts, processes and skills which have been covered by each child. The method of recording the child's level of achievement within each area needs to be agreed between teachers in the school (by ticking, colouring in, etc.). The Progress Records do not preclude detailed records being kept about each child on a day-to-day basis.

Apparatus list
Peak Two

Apparatus
abacus
balance and weights
base 10 MAB materials
beads
bean bags
calculator
cm² transparent grid
compass
counters
digit cards 0 to 9
elastic bands
equaliser balance
funnel
geoboard
interlocking shapes (e.g. Clixi)
jug
kettle
litre container
long tape
marbles
metre stick
mirror
mixing bowl
number grid (100 square)
number rods

peas
peg board
pegs
plane shapes
plastic bottle
plasticine
rice
sand
scissors
set square
small cubes
straws
tape measure
teapot
timer
trundle wheel

Stationery
card
coloured paper
gummed paper
isometric paper*
plain paper*
spotty paper*
squared paper*

* included in *New Peak Stationery Copymasters*, Thomas Nelson and Sons Ltd, 1990.

Index

Answers   Peak Two part 1

Photocopy

page 4

1. 36, 37
2. 89, 90
3. 58, 59
4. 71, 72
5. 25, 26, 27
6. 36, 37, 38
7. 69, 70, 71
8. 125, 126, 127

page 5

Check children's answers

page 6

1. 10
2. 6000
3. 600
4. 60
5. 6000

page 7

1. 3021
2. 4357
3. 4205
4. 5452
5. 6032
6. 4404
7. 6350
8. 7519
9. 3520

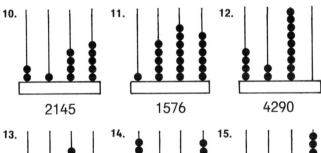

10. 2145   11. 1576   12. 4290

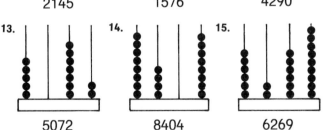

13. 5072   14. 8404   15. 6269

page 8

1. 100, 135, 505, 1000
2. 105, 495, 800, 1010
3. 165, 850, 1065, 1550

4. 340, 925, 1050, 1275
5. 70, 190, 1125, 1390
6. 250, 900, 1400, 3050
7. 40, 120, 350, 1400
8. 15, 445, 770, 1115

page 9

1. even numbers, 310 etc.
2. 13
3. 3100, 3010, 3001, 4000
4. for example: 1111, 1201
5. for example: 1111, 2011
6. for example: 1111, 1210

page 10

1.
6	7	2
1	5	9
8	3	4

2.
8	1	6
3	5	7
4	9	2

3.
4	3	8
9	5	1
2	7	6

page 11

4. If 3 is added to each number it is still a magic square.
5. If each number is multiplied by 5, it is still a magic square.
6. each number has been increased by 5
7. each number has been halved
8. each number has been doubled and 1 added
9. each number has been doubled and 1 subtracted

10.
1	15	14	4
12	6	7	9
8	10	11	5
13	3	2	16

page 12

1. 134	2. 173	3. 174	4. 158
5. 212	6. 291	7. 611	8. 1010

9. 259

10. 398

11. 1044

12. 1114

13. 449

14. 434

15. 712

16. 169

17. 614

18. 1110

19. 487

20. 903

page 13

1.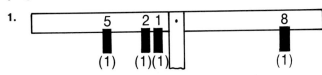

2.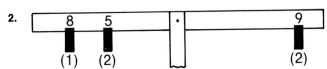

3.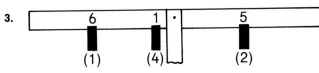

4.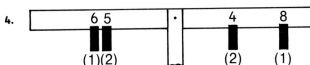

Other combinations are possible.

page 14

Total distance around the shape is 66 cm.

Check children's answers

page 15

1. 34 cm   2. 16 cm

3. 30 cm   4. 36 cm

page 16

1. $12\frac{3}{4}$ m

2. $7\frac{1}{2}$ m

3. 150 cm

4. 25 cm

5. 275 cm

6. $1\frac{1}{2}$ m or 150 cm

7. $4\frac{1}{2}$ m or 450 cm

8. 1000 m

page 17

1. $1\frac{1}{2}$ m

2. $\frac{3}{4}$ m

3. 5

4. 75 cm

5. 1 m

page 20

1. 432	2. 306	3. 965	4. 392	5. 374
6. 725	7. 882	8. 614	9. 844	10. 556
11. 306	12. 645	13. 715	14. 273	15. 587
16. 397	17. 624	18. 466	19. 833	20. 359
21. 492	22. 213	23. 736	24. 109	25. 381

page 21

Check children's answers

page 22

1. (20 − 8) (72 ÷ 6)   (36 − 20) (64 ÷ 4)

   (16 + 8) (48 ÷ 2)   (7 × 2) (98 ÷ 7)

   (10 × 3) (60 ÷ 2)   (17 + 2) (38 ÷ 2)

   (70 ÷ 10) (13 − 6)

2. Check children's answers

page 23

A 122   B 502   C 38   D 816

E 59   F 227   G 125   H 757

I 322   J 32   K 838   L 307

1. B, L
2. A, B, C, D, I, J, K
3. G
4. D, K

page 24

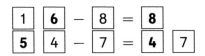

page 25

1. 360, 245
2. 245 and any other
3. 360, 310
4. 294, 245
5. 274, 294
6. 310, 308

pages 26 and 27

1. 65p
2. 1 hour 5 minutes
3. 135
4. 2100 g
5. 600 g
6. £1·30
7. 40 minutes
8. 125 g
9. 519
10. 1500 g

page 28

Check children's answers

page 29

Check children's answers

page 30

Check children's answers

page 31

Check children's answers

page 32

Check children's answers

page 33

1. cow
2. tractor
3. west
4. east

page 34

1. 4 times
2. E
3. S
4. W
5. W
6. W
7. W

page 36

apple, melon, cherry, orange

page 37

There are 41 table answers.

page 38

1. 12
2. 40
3. 20
4. 15
5. 12
6. 18
7. 10
8. 16

page 39

1. 105	2. 176	3. 270	4. 378
5. 185	6. 342	7. 744	8. 176
9. 549	10. 192	11. 546	12. 260
13. 350	14. 252	15. 252	16. 344
17. 735	18. 816	19. 918	20. 849

page 40

1. A, 150 ml   B, 400 ml   C, 300 ml
2. C
3. A, 350 ml   B, 100 ml   C, 200 ml
4. 150 ml
5. 100 ml

page 42

1. $\frac{1}{2}$ shown, $\frac{1}{2}$ missing
2. $\frac{1}{4}$ shown, $\frac{3}{4}$ missing
3. $\frac{3}{4}$ shown, $\frac{1}{4}$ missing
4. $\frac{1}{2}$ shown, $\frac{1}{2}$ missing
5. $\frac{1}{4}$ shown, $\frac{3}{4}$ missing
6. $\frac{3}{4}$ shown, $\frac{1}{4}$ missing
7. $\frac{1}{2}$ shown, $\frac{1}{2}$ missing
8. 1   9. 1   10. $\frac{1}{2}$
11. $\frac{3}{4}$ 12. $\frac{3}{4}$

page 43

1. A, 1   B, $2\frac{1}{2}$ C, $3\frac{1}{2}$
2. A, $\frac{1}{4}$ B, $\frac{3}{4}$ C, $1\frac{1}{2}$
3. A, 4   B, 10   C, 14
4. A, 15   B, 30   C, 35
5. A, $1\frac{1}{2}$ B, $7\frac{1}{2}$ C, $10\frac{1}{2}$
6. A, $7\frac{1}{2}$ B, $12\frac{1}{2}$ C, $17\frac{1}{2}$

page 44

Check children's answers

page 45

Check children's answers

page 46

1. pilchards
2. ketchup
3. sardines
4. No

page 48

1. 38 kg   2. 25 kg
3. 44 kg   4. 32 kg
5. 36 kg   6. 28 kg

page 50

BIRD, NEST
BADGER, SET

page 51

1. 38
2. 39   3. 40   4. 27   5. 72
6. 68   7. 47   8. 33   9. 54
10. 30   11. 17   12. 41   13. 51
14. 56   15. 22   16. 22   17. 14
18. 79   19. 74   20. 143   21. 62

page 52

1. 6
2. 4
3. 3
4. $\frac{1}{6}$ (2 counters), $\frac{1}{12}$ (1 counter)
5. $\frac{1}{2}, \frac{1}{4}, \frac{1}{8}, \frac{1}{3}, \frac{1}{6}, \frac{1}{12}, \frac{1}{24}$

page 53

1. 12
2. 16
3. 20
4. 35
5. 28
6. 24

page 54

1. 15   2. 28
3. $30\frac{1}{2}$ 4. 16
5. 33   6. 20

page 55

1. A, B and D

2. and 3. Check children's work

page 57

The approximate area is

1. 28 squares   2. 23 squares   3. 11 squares
4. 10 squares   5. 16 squares

page 58

1. £1·25
2. £1·05
3. 260
4. 11
5. 86p

page 59

6. 69p
7. John £2·11, Cathryn £1·74
8. John 11p, Cathryn 48p

page 60

1. 75p	2. 30p	3. 55p	4. 95p
5. 32p	6. 64p	7. 73p	8. 88p
9. 36p	10. 8p	11. 12p	12. 26p
13. £2·50	14. £1·55	15. £2·20	
16. £3·64	17. £4·25	18. £2·42	
19. £1·14	20. 7p	21. £1·38	

page 61

1. £1·60, 50p, 22p
2. £4
3. £4·13
4. 20p
5. £3·20
6. 31p
7. Stamps printed are 1p, 2p, 3p, 4p, 5p, 10p, 13p, 18p, 20p, 22p, 24p, 26p, 28p, 31p, 34p, 50p, 75p, £1·00, £1·60, £2·00, £5·00

page 62

1. 9.00 am
2. 12.45 pm
3. 4.30 pm
4. 7.30 am
5. 8.45 pm

page 63

1. 2 hours
2. 3 hours
3. 5 hours
4. 3 hours
5. 4 hours
6. 4 hours
7. 6 hours
8. 7 hours
9. 2 hours, 10 minutes, 30 minutes, 1 hour 50 minutes, 30 minutes, 1 hour 10 minutes, 20 minutes, 30 minutes, 45 minutes
10. International Athletics
11. News at 5.00 pm
12. 30 minutes

page 65

1. 22 February
2. 25 January
3. 1 March
4. 11 March
5. Tuesday
6. No

7. and 8. Check with current calendar

page 67

1. Saturday
2. Wednesday
3. Tuesday and Friday
4. 80
5. Thursday
6. Monday
7. 330 children

8. Sunday

9. Wednesday

10. Children are not at school

Assessment

1. 1722   2. 2402

3. Check answer

4. 500 g

5. 250 ml

6. 35 cm

7. $1\frac{1}{4}$ 8. £1·25

9. 24 cm

10. 216   11. 940   12. 474

13. 273

14. Check children's work

15. NESW

16. A, $\frac{3}{10}$ B, $\frac{5}{10}$ $(\frac{1}{2})$

17. 57   18. 9 r 3   19. 18

20. 4.35   21. 7 × 5

22. Check graph

Answers   Peak Two part 2

Photocopy

page 4

1. 42	2. 28	3. 87	
4. 75	5. 8	6. 15	
7. 73	8. 61	9. 94	10. 3
11. 48	12. 82		
13. 57	14. 69		
15. 115	16. 224	17. 237	18. 318	19. 252
20. 74	21. 150	22. 34	23. 288	24. 165

page 5

1. A	6. 8562
2. C	7. 1827
3. 4198	8. 2431
4. 4371	9. 979
5. 5932	10. 3404

page 6

1. C (1346)
2. C (355)
3. A (992)
4. B (122)

page 7

1.	15 +23 = 38	2.	27 +32 = 59	3.	41 +36 = 77	4.	33 +35 = 68

5.	23 +45 = 68	6.	37 +51 = 88	7.	12 +37 = 49	8.	38 +40 = 78

9.	42 −27 = 15	10.	54 −11 = 43	11.	39 −27 = 12	12.	43 −17 = 26

page 8

squares 1, 4, 9, 16, 25, 36
triangles 1, 4, 9, 16, 25, 36, 49

page 9

A diagonal line
An offset diagonal line

page 10

shape A (20 cm)
shape B 17 cm, shape C 16 cm, shape D 14 cm

page 12

110 cm	1 m 10 cm	1·10 m
206 cm	2 m 6 cm	2·06 m
326 cm	3 m 26 cm	3·26 m
35 cm	35 cm	0·35 m
164 cm	1 m 64 cm	1·64 m
96 cm	96 cm	0·96 m
105 cm	1 m 5 cm	1·05 m

page 15

1. 1 to 2, 3·60 m   2 to 3, 3·30 m
   3 to 4, 1·70 m   4 to 5, 2·90 m
2. 3 and 4
3. 11·50 m
4. car number 2
5. 60 cm

page 16

1. 2998   2. 1000   3. 501   4. 599
5. 990   6. 5994   7. 251   8. 999
9. 250   10. 999   11. 2·50 m   12. 99p   13. $\frac{3}{4}$ l
14. 1398   15. 2998   16. £7·98   17. $4\frac{1}{2}$ kg   18. $3\frac{1}{2}$ m
19. 316
20. 620
21. 999
22. 442
23. 1210
24. 72

page 17

1. 346
2. 285
3. 186
4. 92
5. 69

page 18

1. 350
2. 154
3. 1537
4. 5348
5. 70

page 19

The answer is always 1089.

page 20

There are many solutions. An example for each is given below.

1. $4 \times 5 \times 5$ 2. $84 + 8 + 8$ 3. $91 + 9$
4. $5 \times 5 \times 2 \times 2$
5. $73 + 7 + 3 + 7 + 3 + 7$
6. $20 \times 2 \times 2 + 20$

page 21

There are many solutions. An example for each is given below.

1. $22 + 54 + 10$ 2. $29 + 100 - 7$
3. $49 \times 4 - 49$ 4. $148 - 79 - 10$
5. $102 - 78 + 1$
6. $116 - 42 - 1$ 7. $44 \times 9 - 9$

page 23

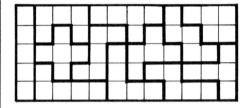

There are other solutions.

page 24

B, C, D, F

page 29

1. less   2. less
3. more   4. less   5. more
6. less

page 30

1.
21	24	27
28	32	36

2.
12	15	18
16	20	24
	25	30

3.
3	4	5
6	8	10
9	12	15

4.
5	6	7
10	12	14
15	18	21
20	24	28
25	30	35

5.
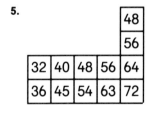

6.
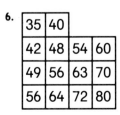

7.
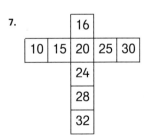

8.

		40	45
		48	54
42	49	56	63
48	56	64	72

19. 350

20. 1100

21. 2947   **22.** 7488   **23.** 9470   **24.** 3552

25. 3580   **26.** 2028   **27.** 8064   **28.** 3805

page 35

Check the children's answers. Possible answers are as follows.

1. $4 \times 5 \times 5$ **2.** $2 \times 5 \times 6$ **3.** $2 \times 4 \times 6$

4. $2 \times 9 \times 3$ **5.** $2 \times 3 \times 11$ **6.** $6 \times 9 \times 2$

7. 5

8. 21

9. 9

10. 36

page 31

1. 760   **2.** 370   **3.** 480   **4.** 290   **5.** 1600

6. 2100   **7.** 4000   **8.** 1360   **9.** 1010   **10.** 1100

11. 34   **12.** 17   **13.** 59   **14.** 140   **15.** 100

16. 203   **17.** 190   **18.** 303   **19.** 270   **20.** 500

21. A and H   B and J   C and K   D and F
E and G   I and L

page 32

When multiplied diagonally, opposite numbers give the same answer.

page 33

1. 1, 2, 3, 4, 6, 12

2. 1, 2, 3, 5, 6, 10, 15, 30

3. 1, 3, 9, 27

4. 1, 2, 4, 8, 16

5. 1, 2, 3, 4, 6, 9, 12, 18, 36

6. 1, 2, 3, 6, 9, 18

7. 1, 2, 4, 8, 16, 32

8. 1, 3, 9

9. 1, 3, 5, 15

10. 1, 2, 4, 5, 10, 20

11. 1, 2, 7, 14

page 34

1. 48   **2.** 63   **3.** 56   **4.** 36

5. 54   **6.** 64   **7.** 42   **8.** 32

9. 49   **10.** 36   **11.** 63   **12.** 72

13. 36   **14.** 27   **15.** 81

16. 1456

17. 2508

18. 4794

page 36

1. 1·800 l   **2.** 1·200 l   **3.** 0·400 l   **4.** 1·500 l

page 39

1. $\frac{1}{8}$ **2.** $\frac{1}{2}$ **3.** $\frac{1}{4}$ **4.** $\frac{5}{8}$

5. $\frac{3}{4}$ **6.** $\frac{7}{8}$ **7.** $\frac{3}{8}$ **8.** 1

page 40

1. $\frac{3}{4}$

2. $\frac{7}{8}$

3. $\frac{1}{2}$

4. $\frac{3}{8}$

5. $\frac{3}{4}$

page 41

1. $\frac{3}{5}$ **2.** $\frac{2}{5}$

page 42

1. $\frac{3}{10}$

2. $\frac{3}{10}$

3. $\frac{4}{10}$ or $\frac{2}{5}$

4. $\frac{1}{5}$

5. $\frac{2}{10}$ **6.** $\frac{4}{10}$ **7.** $\frac{6}{10}$

8. $\frac{8}{10}$ **9.** $\frac{5}{10}$

page 43

1. A, $\frac{2}{5}$ B, $1\frac{4}{5}$
2. A, $\frac{5}{8}$ B, $1\frac{1}{4}$ $(1\frac{2}{8})$
3. A, $\frac{2}{5}$ $(\frac{4}{10})$ B, $1\frac{1}{2}$ $(1\frac{5}{10})$
4. A, $1\frac{1}{4}$ B, $3\frac{1}{2}$ $(3\frac{2}{4})$
5. A, $\frac{1}{10}$ B, $\frac{3}{5}$ $(\frac{6}{10})$ C, $\frac{9}{10}$

page 44

1. $1\frac{9}{10}$ 2. $3\frac{3}{10}$
3. $1\frac{2}{10}$ 4. $\frac{7}{10}$
5. $2\frac{5}{10}$ 6. $7\frac{4}{10}$
7. $3\frac{1}{10}$ 8. $4\frac{8}{10}$
9. $3\frac{6}{10}$ 10. $\frac{8}{10}$

page 45

1. A, 0·3   B, 1·1   C, 1·3   D, 1·5   E, 1·8
2. 2·9, 3·6, 2·6
3. 0·6, 1·4, 0·3, 1·3, 1·1, 0·7

page 46

1. 1·800 kg   2. 2·400 kg   3. 3·600 kg   4. 2·800 kg

page 47

1. 1·650 kg   2. 4·630 kg   3. 2·500 kg
4. 3·490 kg   5. 2·300 kg   6. 1·240 kg
7. 500 g   8. 1250 g   9. 750 g   10. 2500 g
11. 1750 g   12. 2000 g   13. 2750 g   14. 3500 g

page 48

1. 4, 6, 10, 7   2. 4, 10, 8, 9
3. 101   4. 41   5. 147   6. 139
7. 62   8. 87   9. 139   10. 87
11. 91   12. 90   13. 91   14. 73
15. 13   16. 13   17. 12   18. 12
19. 52   20. 242
21. 84   22. 63
23. 51   24. 71
25. 25

page 49

1. A, D, E, H, I, J
2. B, E, F, I
3. $51 \div 8$ as $8)\overline{408}$ 4. 41 as $9)\overline{369}$ 5. 118 as $7)\overline{826}$ 6. 104 as $4)\overline{416}$
7. 66 as $6)\overline{396}$ 8. 71 as $5)\overline{355}$ 9. 61 as $10)\overline{610}$ 10. 223 as $2)\overline{446}$
11. $\begin{array}{r} 33 \\ \times\ 5 \\ \hline 165 \end{array}$ 12. $\begin{array}{r} 103 \\ \times\ 3 \\ \hline 309 \end{array}$ 13. $\begin{array}{r} 17 \\ \times\ 4 \\ \hline 68 \end{array}$ 14. $\begin{array}{r} 114 \\ \times\ 6 \\ \hline 684 \end{array}$

page 50

1. 75   2. 82   3. 37
4. 50   5. 64   6. 16
7. 53   8. 29   9. 78
10. 5   11. 2   12. 5
13. 10   14. 5   15. 10

page 52

1. 12 cm²   2. 12 cm²   3. 12 cm²

page 53

1. 15 cm²   2. 21 cm²
3. 16 cm²   4. 28 cm²
5. 17 cm²   6. 31 cm²

pages 54 and 55

1. approx. 11 cm²   2. approx. 11 cm²
3. approx. 7 cm²   4. approx. 12 cm²
5. approx. 18 cm²   6. approx. 10 cm²
7. approx. 18 cm²   8. approx. 16 cm²
9. approx. 21 cm²   10. approx. 41 cm²
11. approx. 6 cm²   12. approx. 14 cm²

page 56

1. 3p, 4p, 5p, 6p, 7p, 8p, 9p, 11p, 12p, 15p

2. 4p, 5p, 6p, 7p, 8p, 9p, 10p, 11p, 12p, 13p, 14p, 16p, 17p, 20p

3. 4p, 9p, 14p, 19p, 24p, 29p, 34p, 39p, 44p, 49p

page 57
1. £16·80
2. £15·45
3. £14·20
4. open ended

page 58
1. £8·75
2. £9·84
3. £5·40
4. £7·40
5. £31·39

page 59
A £4·92   B £5·17
C £5·06   D £4·77
Bills B and C

page 60
1. 10 minutes
2. 1 hour 35 minutes
3. Old Trafford, Manchester
4. Gardening Today
5. Cartoon Time
6. 50 minutes
7. London Chimes
8. Under fives

page 61
12.15

page 62
1. 1.10   2. 3.25   3. 4.40
4. 5.55   5. 6.15   6. 10.45
7. 12.05   8. 8.35   9. 9.20

page 63
1. 45 minutes   2. 55 minutes   3. 25 minutes
4. 1 hour 40 minutes   5. 1 hour 5 minutes
6. 1 hour 20 minutes
7. 4.30 pm
8. 4.55 pm
9. 5.05 pm   Yes

page 64
1. 3
2. 45 minutes
3. 11.20
4. 11.20
5. 12.05

page 65
1. 4th
2. 469
3. 110
4. 671
5. 4309

page 66
1. No
2. Showers
3. Yes
4. No
5. Scotland
6. Bristol
7. Aberdeen
8. Liverpool, Southampton
9. 7°C
10. Edinburgh

page 67
1. March, November, December
2. June
3. 6 days
4. 17 days
5. 192

Assessment

1. 5574

2. 108

3.
$$\begin{array}{r} 106 \\ \times\ \ 3 \\ \hline 318 \end{array}$$

4.
$$\begin{array}{r} 216 \\ -185 \\ \hline 31 \end{array}$$

5.
$$5\overline{)\,510\,}^{\ \ 102}$$

6. $\frac{3}{8}$ coloured, $\frac{5}{8}$ not coloured

7. $\frac{3}{4}$

8. A, $\frac{5}{10}$ B, $1\frac{6}{10}$

9. 1·600 kg

10. 1·700 l

11. £5·98

12. $3\frac{1}{2}$ kg

13. 1000

14. 350

15. £1·51

16. $1\frac{1}{4}$ l

17. 37 cm

18. $1\frac{9}{10}$

19. $2\frac{2}{10}$

20. $1\frac{1}{2}$

21. 4·8

22. 45 minutes

23. 20 cm²

24. Check children's work

Answers   Number Skills Two

Photocopy

page 4

1

1. 547, 772, 990, 621, 374, 463
2. 972, 1700, 1240, 1192, 864, 1900
3. 1020, 742, 1100, 525, 897, 942

2

C, D

page 5

3

1. 278 + **222**   2. **83** + 417   3. 197 + **303**
4. 354 + **146**   5. **138** + 362   6. **346** + 154
7. 78 + **422**

4

1. 55 + 56   2. 88 + 89   3. 115 + 116
4. 103 + 104   5. 146 + 147   6. 69 + 70

page 6

5

1. (37, 23) (15, 45) (26, 34) (25, 35)
2. (72, 8) (47, 33) (39, 41) (56, 24)

6

1. (76, 74) (92, 58) (88, 62) (36, 114)
2. (110, 190) (160, 140) (170, 130) (180, 120)

7

49

page 7

8

A

64	28	92
98	110	208
162	138	300

B

64	108	172
69	49	118
133	157	290

C

114	69	183
75	42	117
189	111	300

D

126	48	174
67	59	126
193	107	300

E

134	62	196
86	28	114
220	90	310

F

92	106	198
58	44	102
150	150	300

A, C, D and F have totals of 300.

9

22, 64, 60, 84, 28, 79, 8

page 8

10

1. 1146   2. 1223
3. 1311   4. 1184
5. 1486   6. 947

11

1. 385   2. 580
3. 717   4. 870
5. 507   6. 959
7. 634   8. 777

12

1. 1032   2. 616
3. 820   4. 724
5. 481   6. 591

page 9

13

THE BACK OF A CLOCK

14

1. 236   2. 466   3. 376   4. 126
5. 316   6. 146   7. 536   8. 736

15

1. 268   2. 196   3. 389   4. 508
5. 171   6. 434   7. 577   8. 342

page 10

16

1. 234   2. 496   3. 684
  +589   +247   +297
  ―――   ―――   ―――
   823   743   981

4. 328   5. 176   6. 346
  +574   +469   +268
  ―――   ―――   ―――
   902   645   614

17

1. 97, 117
2. 565
3. 117, 97, 242
4. 1081

page 11

18

1. 503   2. 537
3. 775   4. 787
5. 640   6. 954

19

369 + 316 is the odd one out

20

1. 546, 410, 374, 706, 673
2. 776, 930, 677, 895, 700

page 12

21

1. 416   2. 609   3. 594   4. 370
5. 229   6. 208

22

1. 541   2. 755   3. 907   4. 900
5. 706   6. 223
7. 358   8. 636

23

1. 795   2. 463   3. 771   4. 612
5. 913   6. 515   7. 608   8. 817

page 13

24

1. 1103   2. 1260   3. 1318   4. 1274
5. 1124   6. 1070   7. 1302   8. 1251

25

1. 1140   2. 1146
3. 446   4. 1109
5. 1127   6. 1227
7. 1324   8. 1019

26

1. 4096   2. 5791   3. 3859   4. 7429
5. 7450   6. 7551   7. 7794   8. 7584

page 14

27

1. 137, 106, 57, 8, 124, 119
2. 253, 308, 413, 168, 88, 215

28

B, D, E, F, G

page 15

29

1. 165, 76, 264, 460, 353, 696
2. 376, 721, 505, 401, 280, 184, 668

30

592, 149, 656, 201, 773, 484, 628

31

1. 279   2. 687

page 16

32

1. 372 2. 476 3. 552 4. 147 5. 535 6. 318

33

1. 228 2. 274 3. 753 4. 159 5. 249 6. 369

34

1. 378 2. 343 3. 584 4. 533 5. 429 6. 438

35

453

page 17

36

1. 527   2. 554   3. 457   4. 415

37

1. 212   2. 458   3. 486   4. 28

38

1. 226   2. 406   3. 374   4. 343

39

(378, 418) (608, 568) (598, 638) (398, 438)

page 18

40

BECAUSE THEY ARE BATS

41

523 − 356 is the odd one out.

page 19

42

1. 741, 464, 685, 30, 468, 515, 291, 175

2. 3761, 1873, 975, 7.625, 6971, 4490, 5001, 3924

43

£0·76

page 20

44

A, B, D, G, H, I

page 21

45

1. 742 − 394 = 348
2. 901 − 278 = 623
3. 342 − 196 = 146
4. 700 − 247 = 453
5. 856 − 198 = 658
6. 639 − 492 = 147
7. 607 − 248 = 359
8. 411 − 223 = 188

46

1. 449
2. 211
3. C (397)
4. 134

page 22

47

1. 223   2. 23   3. 145
4. 47   5. 225   6. 218

48

1. 556 2. 549 3. 376 4. 208
5. 229 6. 117 7. 158 8. 236

49

1. 58   2. 177   3. 475
4. 368   5. 163   6. 258
7. 586   8. 185   9. 338

50

1. 164   2. 254   3. 653   4. 166
5. 348   6. 249   7. 464   8. 29

page 23

51

1. 732   2. 1713   3. 2932   4. 1612
5. 4728   6. 3846   7. 3918   8. 1819

52

1. 5291   2. 3127
3. 2743   4. 4656

53

1. 2128   2. 3092   3. 3782   4. 1439
5. 2575   6. 1276   7. 1868   8. 5551
9. 1573   10. 6058   11. 7588   12. 3574

page 24

54

$7 \times 4 = \boxed{28}$ $\boxed{2} \times 7 = 14$
$\boxed{8} \times 7 = 56$ $10 \times \boxed{7} = 70$
$5 \times \boxed{7} = 35$ $7 \times 9 = \boxed{63}$
$\boxed{7} \times 2 = 14$ $3 \times \boxed{7} = 21$
$6 \times 7 = \boxed{42}$ $\boxed{7} \times 8 = 56$

55

×6 table
12, 30, 54 are missing.

56

×3 table: 9, 24, 18, 15, 27, 12
×8 table: 24, 64, 16, 40, 72, 48

page 25

57

56	54	40
20	42	63
54	36	40
15	12	30
63	0	72
24	49	64

58

1.
×	2	7	8
4	8	28	32
5	10	35	40
3	6	21	24

2.
×	9	2	6
7	63	14	42
3	27	6	18
8	72	16	48

59

36 years

page 26

60

×7 table
7, 21, 42, 70 are missing.

61

$6 \times \boxed{3} = 18$ $5 \times 9 = \boxed{45}$
$7 \times 4 = \boxed{28}$ $7 \times \boxed{5} = 35$
$\boxed{9} \times 6 = 54$ $\boxed{10} \times 3 = 30$
$\boxed{8} \times 8 = 64$ $9 \times \boxed{9} = 81$
$3 \times \boxed{9} = 27$ $8 \times 7 = \boxed{56}$

62

×7 table: 14, 35, 56, 49, 63
×9 table: 45, 36, 72, 81, 90, 63, 27

page 27

63

513 × 7 is the odd one out. It is the only one
with an odd answer.

64

140, 180, 70, 285, 400, 245, 310, 470

65

854, 1264, 1034, 570, 758, 1248, 1118

page 28

66

144 × 9 is the odd one out. It is the only one which does not end in 0.

67

1. 168 bottles
2. 180, 248, 716, 224, 376, 288, 336, 956

page 29

68

TO FEED HIS NIGHTMARE

page 30

69

1. 234, 744, 468, 1482, 1974, 582, 1008, 510
2. 770, 1195, 370, 960, 1725, 1315, 470, 415

70

1. 234 × 5 = 1170	2. 775 × 6 = 4650	3. 456 × 4 = 1824	4. 504 × 9 = 4536
5. 727 × 7 = 5089	6. 349 × 3 = 1047	7. 812 × 8 = 6496	8. 746 × 5 = 3730
9. 439 × 10 = 4390	10. 674 × 2 = 1348	11. 593 × 7 = 4151	12. 473 × 9 = 4257

page 31

71

2436, 5544, 1022, 4081, 2058, 2849, 4389, 3325

72

A, 2576   B, 3807   C, 890   D, 1896
E, 2781   F, 5488   G, 2422   H, 2655
I, 4350   J, 1960

page 32

73

1. 294	2. 435	3. 432	4. 162
5. 312	6. 380	7. 440	8. 56

74

1. 273	2. 420	3. 168
4. 470	5. 424	6. 738
7. 216	8. 273	9. 196
10. 616	11. 129	12. 270

75

1. 276	2. 430	3. 174	4. 480
5. 352	6. 657	7. 228	8. 266

page 33

76

1. 3073	2. 2104	3. 3444	4. 1032
5. 6858	6. 745	7. 2355	8. 4560

77

1. 5416	2. 590	3. 1026
4. 4470	5. 3321	6. 1337
7. 6984	8. 670	9. 2709
10. 3568	11. 3222	12. 2472

78

1. 3915	2. 1716	3. 7710	4. 1464
5. 6860	6. 2715	7. 2232	8. 6903

page 34

79

$60 \div 7, 22 \div 6, 40 \div 9, 44 \div 5, 76 \div 9,$
$68 \div 8$

80

$63 \div 7 = \boxed{9}$ $15 \div \boxed{3} = 5$ $18 \div \boxed{6} = 3$
$25 \div 5 = \boxed{5}$ $24 \div 3 = \boxed{8}$ $35 \div \boxed{7} = 5$
$32 \div \boxed{4} = 8$ $54 \div 9 = \boxed{6}$ $48 \div 6 = \boxed{8}$
$40 \div 5 = \boxed{8}$ $42 \div \boxed{6} = 7$ $36 \div 4 = \boxed{9}$
$72 \div \boxed{8} = 9$ $27 \div 3 = \boxed{9}$ $32 \div \boxed{8} = 4$
$45 \div \boxed{9} = 5$ $81 \div \boxed{9} = 9$ $49 \div \boxed{7} = 7$

81

$42 \div \boxed{7} = 6$ is the odd one out.

page 35

82

1. $32 \div \boxed{8}$
$\dfrac{24}{\boxed{6}} = 4$
$\boxed{9}\,\overline{)36}$

2. $\boxed{9}\,\overline{)54}$
$\dfrac{24}{\boxed{4}} = 6$
$30 \div \boxed{5}$

3. $\dfrac{72}{\boxed{8}}$
$45 \div \boxed{5} = 9$
$\boxed{7}\,\overline{)63}$

4. $\boxed{8}\,\overline{)56}$
$\dfrac{35}{\boxed{5}} = 7$
$21 \div \boxed{3}$

5. $\boxed{56} \div 7$
$\dfrac{72}{\boxed{9}} = 8$
$\boxed{6}\,\overline{)48}$

page 36

83

1. $\boxed{136} \div 8$ $\boxed{85} \div 5 = 17$ $\boxed{51} \div 3$

2. $\boxed{78} \div 6$ $\boxed{52} \div 4 = 13$ $\boxed{117} \div 9$

3. $\boxed{38} \div 2$ $\boxed{190} \div 10 = 19$ $\boxed{133} \div 7$

4. $\boxed{80} \div 5$ $\boxed{144} \div 9 = 16$ $\boxed{128} \div 8$

84

1. 43   2. 9

85

102, 138, 210, 192, 114, 162

page 37

86

1. 92, 69, 46
2. 85, 34, 68
3. 96, 80, 160

87

1. 42, 28, 63
2. 32, 24, 48
3. 54, 81, 18

page 38

88

1. 19, 13, 26, 38, 22, 46, 40, 28
2. 17, 23, 14, 18, 19, 13   3. 19, 24, 13, 29, 27, 32

89

4. 37   5. 17

90

$90 \div 5$ is the odd one out.

page 39

91

CLIMB OVER WALLS

92

34, 76, 56, 38, 58, 90, 72, 52

page 40

93

1. $7\overline{)203}$ = 29
2. $8\overline{)376}$ = 47
3. $5\overline{)280}$ = 56
4. $3\overline{)252}$ = 84
5. $9\overline{)567}$ = 63
6. $4\overline{)316}$ = 79
7. $6\overline{)276}$ = 46
8. $9\overline{)351}$ = 39
9. $7\overline{)525}$ = 75
10. $8\overline{)464}$ = 58

page 41

94

20

95

1. $1296 \div 3$ = 432 $\div 8$ = 54 $\div 9$ = 6

2. $882 \div 6$ = 147 $\div 7$ = 21 $\div 3$ = 7

96

1. 76, 112, 204, 140, 244
2. 126, 273, 182, 350, 266

page 42

97

1. 14   2. 24   3. 14   4. 13
5. 23   6. 35   7. 17   8. 27
9. 16   10. 12   11. 19   12. 13

98

1. 9   2. 38   3. 15
4. 12   5. 11   6. 27
7. 13   8. 19   9. 22

99

1. 14   2. 15   3. 11   4. 32
5. 42   6. 13   7. 17   8. 12
9. 19   10. 49   11. 15   12. 11

page 43

100

1. 36   2. 54   3. 86   4. 113
5. 132   6. 89   7. 76   8. 258
9. 459   10. 257   11. 153   12. 106

101

1. 148   2. 129   3. 76
4. 84   5. 187   6. 469
7. 138   8. 117   9. 68

102

1. 79   2. 387   3. 156   4. 217
5. 106   6. 315   7. 237   8. 119
9. 104   10. 198   11. 93   12. 294

page 44

103

1. 111, 119, 127
2. 175, 182, 189
3. 101, 107, 113

104

1. 112   2. 60   3. 74

105

423, 176

page 45

106

740, 950, 1130, 870, 1530, 920, 2490, 5760, 1780

107

1. 424   2. 157   3. 324

4. 173   5. 132   6. 178

7. 450   8. 147   9. 551

108

1.

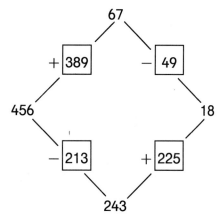

2.

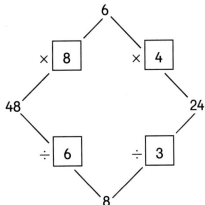

page 46

109

```
  286              834
×   7            +674
─────            ─────
 2002 largest    1508 smallest
```

110

1. 19, 4

2. 7, 19

3. 4, 64

4. 7, 64, 4

page 47

111

A PENGUIN ON A POGO STICK

112

9, 13

page 48

113

H

114

1. 49 + **23**   2. 4 × **18**

3. 301 − **229**   4. **432** ÷ 6

5. **39** + 33   6. **8** × 9

7. **121** − 49   8. **360** ÷ 5

Answers   Peak Explorer Two part 1

Photocopy

page 2

page 3

$10 \times 2 = 5 \times \boxed{4}$ $26 + 38 = \boxed{8} \times 8$

$9 \times \boxed{9} = 100 - 19$ $36 \div 9 = \boxed{32} \div 8$

$12 + 20 - 4 = 7 \times \boxed{4}$ $60 \div 2 = 5 \times \boxed{6}$

The last four examples are open-ended.

Solutions could include:

$60 - 10 - 5 = \boxed{9} \times \boxed{5}$

$12 + 11 + 4 = \boxed{9} \times \boxed{3}$

$50 - \boxed{15} = 5 \times \boxed{7}$

$35 + 28 = \boxed{7} \times \boxed{9}$

page 4

Possible solutions include:

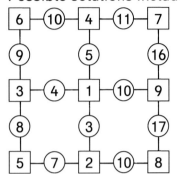

Check that the child has arranged the digit cards to match the totals.

page 5

The answers are open ended. Check the children's answers. Possible solutions include:

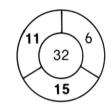
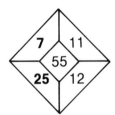

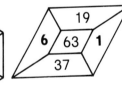
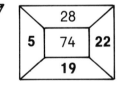

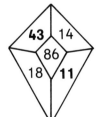
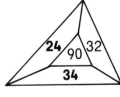
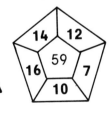

page 6

Check that the grid is divided into four parts and that each part has one of each shape. Possible solutions include:

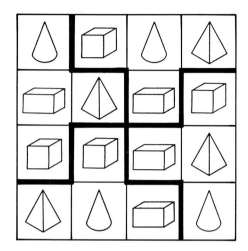

Check that all the columns add up to 40. Possible solutions include:

7	18	15	19
14	2	9	8
6	16	5	3
13	4	11	10

Possible solutions to the matchstick problems include:

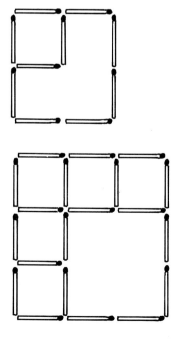

page 7

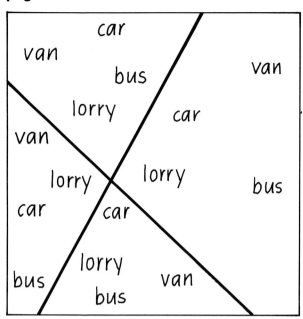

Check that only one straight line has been drawn and that each shape is cut in half.

Possible solutions include:

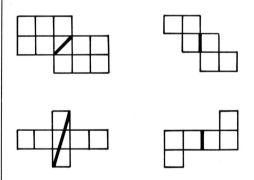

page 8

Answers to examples:

28, 72, 90

42, 56, 49

78, 45, 57

78, 48, 44

Check that the solutions made up match the respective answers.

page 9

120, 131, 131, 175

The last signpost is worth most (175).

pages 10 and 11

Check that each 'domino four' matches its total.

page 12

```
R U F O R T Y F O U R E
B T H E R T Y B O O R A
N H S E V E N T Y T W O
I I S B P F L G N P N R
N R E S E V E N T Y I N
E T L F D J L K N H N I
T Y E O S X V C E O E N
Y F V R D W R B I Z T E
N O E T N Q B L Y O Y T
I U N Y F I F T E E N E
N R E I G H T A R Y V E
E T W E N T Y F I V E N
```

The other number in the searcher is ELEVEN. Check the sum made up to give the answer eleven.

page 13

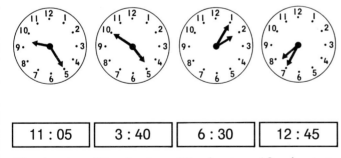

| 11 : 05 | 3 : 40 | 6 : 30 | 12 : 45 |

60 minutes 30 minutes 55 minutes 40 minutes

page 14

OIL

345, SHE   771, ILL

514, HIS   637, LEG

607, LOG   663, EGG

Check the accuracy of the sums made up to give the words IS and LIE.

page 15

TIGER, 59   HORSE, 65

MONKEY, 83   LEOPARD, 71

ELEPHANT, 81   KANGAROO, 82

MONKEY is worth the most (83).

page 16

220, 31, 310, 112

Answers   Peak Explorer Two part 2

Photocopy

page 2

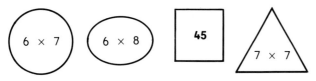

6 × 7   6 × 8   45   7 × 7

63   64

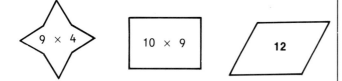

9 × 4   10 × 9   12

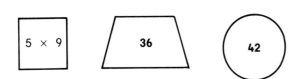

5 × 9   36   42

90   48

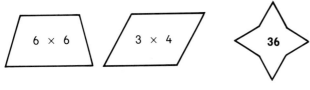

6 × 6   3 × 4   36

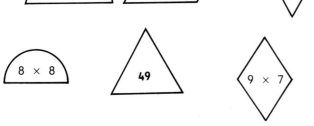

8 × 8   49   9 × 7

page 3

	12	16
10	15	20
12		

40	48	56	64
	54	63	
		70	

6	12	18
7	14	21
8	16	
9	18	

56	64	72	
63	72	81	
	90	100	

					48	54
21	28	35	42	49		
24	32	40	48	56		

page 4

Check that the route taken totals over 100.

Possible solutions include:

```
START → 12 → 10      16      11
                ↓
        9       5      17 → 13
                ↓       ↑      ↓        (Total 107)
        6       8 → 10         14
                                ↓
        7      11      12      18
                               FINISH
```

Check that the route totals exactly 100.

Possible solutions include:

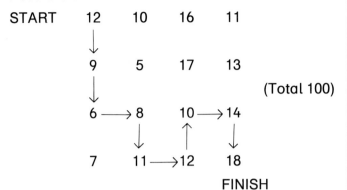

START   12   10   16   11

9   5   17   13

(Total 100)

6 ⟶ 8   10 ⟶ 14

7   11 ⟶ 12   18

FINISH

Check that each part of the grid totals 20.

Possible solutions include:

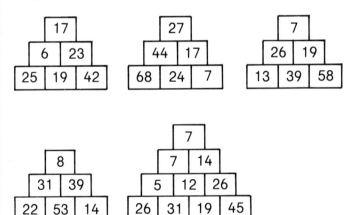

7	4	3	5
2	6	7	8
3	8	1	6

page 5

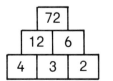

	17	
6	23	
25	19	42

	27	
44	17	
68	24	7

	7	
26	19	
13	39	58

	8	
31	39	
22	53	14

	7		
7	14		
5	12	26	
26	31	19	45

	72	
12	6	
4	3	2

	72	
12	6	
6	2	3

	160	
16	10	
8	2	5

	189	
9	21	
3	3	7

	144	
8	18	
4	2	9

	192	
24	8	
6	4	2

page 6

Possible solutions include:

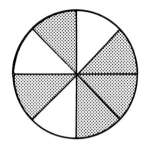

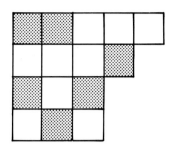

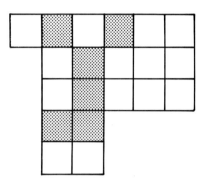

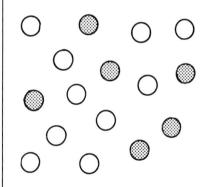

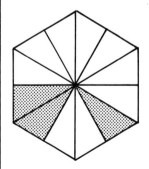

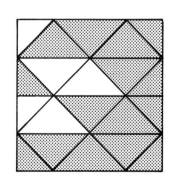

page 7

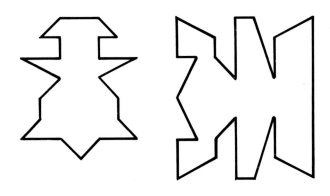

page 8

Check that the child has arranged the digit cards to match the differences.
Possible solutions include:

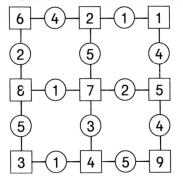

page 9

The mouse gets her dinner in the haystack.

page 10

Check that only the digits 7 and 9 have been used to reach the targets.
Possible solutions include:

$7 \times 7 + 7 + 7 + 7 - 9 - 9 = 52$

$9 + 9 + 7 = 25$

$7 + 7 + 7 + 7 + 9 = 37$

$7 \times 9 + 9 - 7 - 7 = 58$

$9 + 9 + 9 - 7 = 20$

$9 + 9 + 9 - 7 - 7 - 7 = 6$

$9 + 9 + 9 + 9 + 9 - 7 = 38$

$9 + 9 + 9 + 7 = 34$

$7 \times 7 + 7 + 9 = 65$

page 11

Check that the counters at the corners of the shape match the totals.
Possible solutions include:

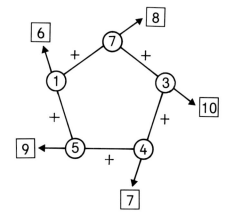

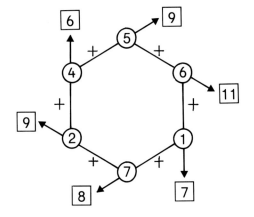

page 12

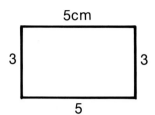

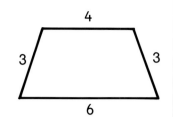

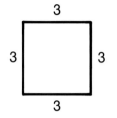

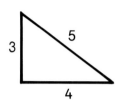

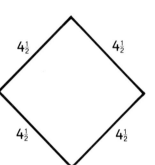

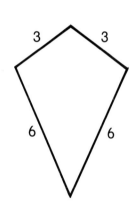

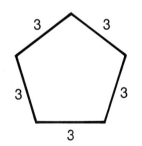

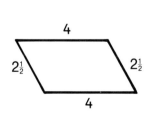

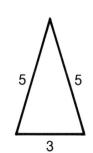

page 13

BIKE   TOY   HAT   BOX   WAIT

page 14

16	29	17
21	11	12
+13	+14	+24
50	54	53

23	13	17
13	16	19
+46	+22	+26
82	51	62

16	6	22
8	12	6
+18	+16	+ 9
42	34	37

14	14	24
6	13	16
+18	+ 4	+18
38	31	58

page 15

6 : 40	7 : 20	8 : 00	8 : 40
3 : 25	4 : 05	4 : 45	5 : 25
12 : 50	1 : 30	2 : 10	2 : 50

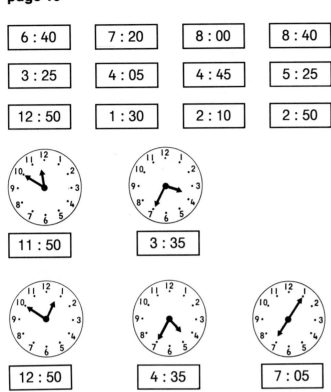

11 : 50   3 : 35

12 : 50   4 : 35   7 : 05

page 16

APPLE   GRAPE   PEAR   ORANGE
PINEAPPLE